MW01484289

PROTECT YOUR WRITINGS
A Legal Guide for Authors

PROTECT YOUR WRITINGS

A Legal Guide for Authors

Maria Crimi Speth

©2010, 2018 Jaburg & Wilk, P.C.
No part of this book may be reproduced in any manner without written permission of the author

The author has used fictitious names in the examples of this book and has sometimes changed the facts of real-life situations in order to illustrate the legal principals.

This book addresses general legal concepts. Every situation will vary depending on the facts. Thus, it is always a good practice to consult with an attorney regarding your specific legal questions.

The trademarks referred to in this book are the property of their respective owners.

ISBN: 9781718121683

Dedication

For my husband Ray
and my children Topher and Nicole

"The Congress shall have power to ... promote the progress of science and useful arts, by securing for limited times to authors and inventors the exclusive right to their respective writings and discoveries... [and] to make all laws which shall be necessary and proper for carrying into execution the foregoing powers..."

-- The United States Constitution, Article 1, Section 8

Acknowledgements

Everything that I do in my life is directly and completely the result of being raised by my amazing mother who found herself the widowed parent of two young children when she was only 42 years old. Thank you, Mom, for always putting our needs before yours and creating the foundation on which my success rests.

I am also eternally grateful to my brother, Steven. Your support and guidance never faltered, even in the face of my young and rebellious refusal to be guided. You have since become my friend and my confidant. I could not have chosen a better big brother.

Speaking of choice, I was fortunate enough to choose and hold onto my soul mate, Ray. I am so very thankful to you for everything that you do. Ray, you are the "wind beneath my wings."

A special "thank you" to my children, Topher and Nicole. You tolerated my late nights and missed dinners and you hardly complained at all while sitting on the curb downtown waiting for me to pick you up. You are beautiful, brilliant, and funny. If I had been given a checklist to create the perfect children, you would be exactly who you are. I am so incredibly proud of both of you.

Thank you to all of the attorneys at Jaburg & Wilk; to Brenda Edwards and to Gary Jaburg for supporting me in my work and in this project. Like Gary always says, "There is nothing better than really liking the people you work with."

A special thanks to CEO Space, a place where entrepreneurs do business in cooperation. Thank you for giving me and the other instructors a place to tithe our knowledge to others. Thank you for giving the members a place to gain the knowledge and contacts needed for success. The Space is magic.

TABLE OF CONTENTS

INTRODUCTION

I have been teaching entrepreneurs the importance of, and how to protect, their intangible assets for more than twenty years. Over the years, many participants in my seminars have encouraged me to write a book on the subject. This book is the synthesis of almost thirty years of working in this field. My goal is to help the reader avoid common mistakes and benefit from the experience of those who have already been through the process.

Protect Your Writings is intended to be the first in a series of books about protecting creative works. The series will include a book for graphic artists, photographers, and songwriters and musicians.

Protect Your Writings is designed to help writers and authors. It is a comprehensive, and yet easy to understand guide that covers all of the "need to know" areas of the law for authors. Whether you are a seasoned author working with a traditional publisher or a new author who is self-publishing your first book, this guide will help you to practice your craft with far less risk. Whether you are working full time in the field or writing as a hobby in your spare time, you will find the information in this book helpful and interesting.

The first chapter covers the four main areas of intellectual property law and the interplay between those areas; all as it relates to authors. The next two chapters focus on copyright law, the main area of law protecting the written word. Chapter 4 discusses trademark law and its application to written works. Chapter 5 walks you through the copyright registration process in detail.

Chapters 6 through 8 provide the perspective of respecting the rights of others to avoid legal claims against you. Chapter 9 addresses international rights and Chapter 10 explains how these concepts apply in an online context. Finally, Chapter 11 covers the contracts that authors are most likely to encounter.

Protect Your Writings is designed to be read from cover to cover, and also as a resource to look up a particular legal issue using the index. To help find the answer to a particular question, the chapters are separated into headings and sometimes subheadings. I encourage you to grab a highlighter and a pen and annotate the sections that you expect to refer to as you encounter future issues. I also encourage you to use this book as a guide to help you identify the issues that you should discuss directly with an attorney.

It is my sincere hope that this guide will help make your writing career more successful. Happy reading!

Chapter 1
Intellectual Property

Since intellectual property law protects our work, it is the most important area of the law for authors to understand. To define intellectual property, we first focus on its legal status as a type of property. Like any other property, it is owned by a person or entity and can be bought, sold, lent, and bequeathed. Like other types of property, intellectual property has value and, indeed, may be a business's most valuable property.

The grandmother of one of my clients had written

hundreds of poems that she gave to my client shortly before she died. The poems were powerful and insightful and my client immediately recognized that they were potentially commercially viable. Since my client has an entrepreneurial streak, she began crafting a business plan to commercialize the poems. She naturally assumed that since she owned the physical poems (they were gifted to her), she had the legal right to reproduce them. But the copyrights in the poems are different property than the physical poems. Although she owned the physical poems, her intellectual property rights were more complicated. Copyrights can only be transferred by written assignment, so her grandmother still owned the copyrights at the time of her death. Because intellectual property is property, we analyzed the ownership of the copyrights like the other property owned by her grandmother when she died. If her grandmother had a will, we would have looked for mention of the copyrights to poems in the will. If they were not specifically mentioned, then we would have looked for the provision of the will that dealt with all of the assets that were not itemized, and the copyrights would be owned by whoever inherited those assets. Since her grandmother did not have a will, we had to look at the law of her grandmother's state of residence to determine the way that assets passed to survivors of those who did not have a will. Once we determined who owned the copyrights to the poems (in her case it was her mother and her mother's sister), I drafted an assignment agreement to transfer ownership in the copyrights of the poems from my client's mother and aunt to my client. It was agreed that they would give up their ownership rights in exchange for a small percentage of the revenue earned from the sale of the poems. They also could have agreed to an up-front payment or no compensation.

Another option could have been for my client's mother and aunt to license, rather than sell, the copyrights to my client. Licensing intellectual property is the equivalent of leasing. You have the right to use it, but you are not the owner. Under a license, my client's mother and her aunt would have retained some degree of control and may have had the right to terminate the license. Of course, my client preferred outright ownership and was willing to pay a little higher compensation to get it.

Understanding that intellectual property is a type of property gets you halfway to understanding how it works. The other half of the definition is the "intellectual" part of intellectual property. A common joke that I hear when I tell people that I am an intellectual property attorney is, "Does that mean you're smart?" I usually joke back and say, "That is exactly what it means." Then I explain that the "intellectual" in intellectual property is actually another word for intangible. Intangible items are those that you cannot touch and feel or hold in your hands.

Intellectual property is the intangible or intellectual aspect of what is otherwise a tangible product. You purchased this book; we call it a purchase because you are now the new *owner* of the *tangible* aspects of the book-the parts you can touch. Essentially, you own the paper. However, when you purchased this book, you did not purchase the intellectual property. Instead, you licensed that aspect from the author. Differentiating between the portions of a work that are owned by the "purchaser" and those portions that are merely licensed by the "purchaser" is one of the most often misunderstood aspects of intellectual property law.

In our loose vocabulary, we tend to refer to everything as selling or a sale. As authors, we need to remember that we rarely sell our intellectual property rights. Rather, we sell the tangible manifestations of our story (the books), and we license the copyrights with limitations.

Intellectual property is comprised of four main areas of law: (1) Copyrights; (2) Trademarks; (3) Trade secrets; and (4) Patents. Some would argue that privacy rights and publicity rights are also intellectual property. While it is not clear whether privacy and publicity rights are technically encompassed under the umbrella of intellectual property, it is clear that authors should be familiar with privacy and publicity rights.

(1) Copyrights

Copyrights are a bundle of legal rights belonging to the owner of an original work of authorship. Copyrights not only cover writings, they also cover musical works, dramatic works, choreographic works, pictorial works, graphic works, sculptural works, and audiovisual works. The copyright to a work covers its content. There must be a sufficient amount of original authorship for there to be copyright protection. Copyrights generally do not cover titles or one-line quotes because there is not a sufficient amount of original content to protect under copyright laws. Since copyrights are the area of law most pertinent to authors, they will be extensively covered in future chapters.

(2) Trademarks

Trademarks identify the source of goods or services. A trademark can be a word, a phrase, a picture, a color, a sound or even a smell. You know it is a trademark if it tells you that the goods or services emanate from a particular source. It is essentially a brand identifier. For example, the company United Parcel Service or UPS owns several well-known trademarks. Among its trademarks are United Parcel Service, the UPS logo (which resembles a gift box), UPS, the color brown on delivery trucks, the color brown for uniforms, and the tag line "What can brown do for you?" United Parcel Services owns each of these trademarks in connection with delivery services.

Trademark rights arise from use of a trademark in connection with certain goods or services. No registration is required to acquire trademark rights in the geographic trade area of your use. Trademarks can be registered at both the state and the federal levels. Trademark registration is not mandatory, but it provides many benefits that common law usage does not provide. Registration on the federal level is particularly important and will actually preempt state registrations.

When you register a trademark with the United States Patent and Trademark Office, you prevent anyone else from registering the same or a confusingly similar trademark in connection with the same or similar goods or services. You also obtain the right to prevent others from using the trademark anywhere in the United States. An exception is that if someone else began their use before you filed for your federal registration, they can continue to use their trademark in their own geographic trade area (but they may not expand beyond the trade area they had when you filed your trademark application).

An example that is well known in the trademark world is Weiner King. Between 1962 and 1975, Weiner King opened three hot dog restaurants in and around Flemington, New Jersey. A second company, also doing business as Weiner King (we'll call this company Weiner King II) opened a hot dog restaurant in 1970 in North Carolina. By 1972, Weiner King II had opened eleven restaurants and it registered its trademark federally. After extensive litigation, the court determined that Weiner King got to keep its trademark in a fifteen-mile radius around Flemington, New Jersey and that Weiner King II was entitled to the trademark for the rest of the United States. Even though Weiner King II was the second user of the trademark, it was the first to file for the federal registration. Its federal registration gave it nationwide rights, except for the trade area established by Weiner King before Weiner King II filed for its federal registration.

One way to spot a trademark, or to know its status, is by the symbols that are used in connection with trademarks. A person or company that claims trademark rights in a word, phrase, or graphic has the right to use the ™ symbol. No registration or application to register is required for use of the ™ symbol. If the trademark owner has actually registered the trademark with the United States Patent & Trademark Office, the owner should use the ® symbol with the trademark. However, if no symbol is used, it does not necessarily mean that no one claims trademark rights in the mark. Use of the symbols is recommended but not mandatory.

Trademarks can sometimes cover the same item as copyrights. Tony the Tiger is a registered trademark of Kellogg's. He is a trademark because he identifies Kellogg's Frosted Flakes. He is also protected by copyright laws because the artistic rendering of Tony the Tiger has enough original authorship to entitle it to such protection.

In Chapter 4, we will more fully explore trademarks as they relate to authors and publishing.

(3) Trade Secrets

Trade secret is an area of law important to know if you have an idea, a plot, or other information which is valuable or potentially valuable and not known to others. Trade secrets are protected by sharing them on a need-to-know basis and then obtaining a signed confidentiality or non-disclosure agreement (NDA) from those who need to know. There is no registration process and availing yourself of the trade secret laws requires nothing more than prudence on your part. Trade secrets are governed by state laws as well as federal law. The law for trademarks, copyrights and patents is the same throughout the United States because they are governed by federal law. Trade secrets, on the other hand, can be treated a bit differently depending on your state of residence. The Uniform Trade Secret Act is a model law that has been adopted in some form by every state except Massachusetts and New York. Because many states adopted a modified version, it is important to remember that the law can differ from state to state.

The Uniform Trade Secrets Act defines a trade secret as information, including a formula, pattern, compilation, program, device, method, technique, or process, that:

(i) derives independent economic value, actual or potential, from not being generally known to, and not being readily ascertainable by proper means, by other persons who can obtain economic value from its disclosure or use, and

(ii) is the subject of efforts that are reasonable under the circumstances to maintain its secrecy.[1]

In 2016, the Federal Defend Trade Secrets Act was passed, adding a federal law option for enforcing trade secrets. The Act's definition of misappropriation is modeled on the Uniform Trade Secret Act. Specifically, trade secret is defined as: "all forms and types of financial, business, scientific, technical, economic, or engineering information, including patterns, plans, compilations, program devices, formulas, designs, prototypes, methods, techniques, processes, procedures, programs, or codes, whether tangible or intangible, and whether or how stored, compiled, or memorialized physically, electronically, graphically, photographically, or in writing if (A) the owner thereof has taken reasonable measures to keep such information secret; and (B) the information derives independent economic value, actual or potential, from not being generally known to, and not being readily ascertainable through proper means by, another person who can obtain economic value from the disclosure or use of the information."

Trade secrets can be important to authors in protecting plots, manuscripts and outlines before they are available to the public. It is also important to understand how trade secret law applies to the protection of your marketing and business plans or any other process or technique that you have created where the value is in the concept, process or technique rather than in the expression.

Trade secret law is the easiest area of intellectual property to understand. Essentially, if you mark the information confidential, share the information on a need-to-know basis, and obtain non-disclosure agreements from anyone who receives the information, then the law will protect you if someone misappropriates the information from you or from someone who was bound by your non-disclosure agreement.

Trade secret law can be used to protect information either on a temporary or on a permanent basis. You may only need to keep something confidential until it can be launched. For example, the plot for a new book or script should be kept confidential until the book is published. On the other hand, trade secrets can be long term or even permanent. The most famous trade secret is the Coca-cola® formula, which has been kept secret for over a hundred years.

Let's say you wake up in the middle of the night with the most incredible idea for a novel. You just know it will be a best-seller. At this point, it is just a concept, so there is nothing to copyright yet. You need some assistance researching the plot, so the next day you call an old high school friend that works in that field. How you handle that telephone call could determine whether trade secret law will protect you. If you tell your friend that what you are about to share is confidential and you ask her to commit to keeping it that way, you have probably acted reasonably to protect your trade secret. Since she is a close friend, it is likely reasonable for you to get her commitment only verbally. To be even safer, and certainly if this is not someone that you know you can trust, you would have her sign a non-disclosure agreement. On the other hand, if you call your friend and a dozen other people and share your exciting news without ever mentioning that it is confidential, you have probably lost any chance of trade secret law protection. Under the law, if you are not careful to keep the information confidential, then the law will not protect you if someone else writes the book before you write it.

One other aspect of trade secret law that every author should know is that often you must choose between copyright protection and trade secret protection. If you have just developed a new food processing method that preserves food without chemicals, how do you best protect that process? Writing a book about it, registering the copyright, and publicizing the book will destroy any chance of keeping that process a trade secret. Copyright law will protect the expression of the idea, but not the idea itself. To protect the food processing method, you will choose between trade secret protection and patent protection. Later, we will analyze those options more fully.

(4) Patents

The final area of intellectual property is patent law. A patent for an invention is the grant of a property right to the inventor, issued by the United States Patent and Trademark Office. It is the "right to exclude others from making, using, offering for sale, or selling"[2] the invention in the United States or "importing" the invention into the United States. A patent may be granted to anyone who invents any new and useful process, machine, manufacture, or composition of matter, or any new or useful improvement thereof."[3] There are also design patents, which may be granted to anyone who invents a new, original, and ornamental design for an article of manufacture.

Generally, patents last for 20 years from the date on which the application for the patent was filed and then they expire and the invention goes into the public domain.

The Interplay Between the Four Areas of Intellectual Property

The interplay between the areas of intellectual property law is important. Not only is it important to understand the definitions and the differences, but it is important to know which type of intellectual property will provide the best protection for your situation.

Often, students of intellectual property law understand the four areas but have difficulty determining which type of intellectual property best protects the work. This is partly because there are times when more than one area of intellectual property applies to a single work and other times when protecting a work under one area of intellectual property completely precludes the protection from another area. For example, a picture is protected by trademark law if it is a logo that is associated with a product or service. A picture is also generally protected by copyright law. On the other hand, you can never get trade secret protection over an invention that you have patented because trade secret protection derives from not being generally known while patent protection requires full public disclosure.

As I do with new clients, let me walk you through the analysis necessary to determine the best protection for your work. The first question that you want to ask yourself is, "What am I doing that is unique?" Consider what you are doing that is different from what others before you have done. Once we identify what sets you apart from others, we can identify what is valuable, which then tells us what needs protection and how to protect it. Your answer may be that *the way* you are describing something is unique or it may be that *what* you are describing is unique. Perhaps both what you are writing about and your description are unique.

If your answer is that only your *description* is unique, then the value of your work lies in your words. In that case, the best protection for your work is copyright law.

If your answer is that *what* you are writing about is unique, then ask yourself, "Is my concept, idea, process or method capable of being kept confidential?" Of course, you want to be able to keep it confidential while still commercializing or monetizing it. If the answer is yes, then you should not write about the confidential aspect of your work and you should look to trade secret law to protect you. If the answer is no, it cannot be kept confidential, then you should review the criteria for obtaining a patent and determine whether patent law may protect your work.

It is entirely possible that neither copyright law, trade secret law nor patent law protect a unique and valuable aspect of your work. It may be impossible to write about the subject without revealing the confidential aspects and it may also be that what you are writing about does not fall into the strict criteria of a patentable work. In that case, you may choose to write about it anyway even though the concept will be revealed and others may utilize your concepts. At least you can commercialize your writings and earn recognition for your work and revenue through book sales.

While not generally applicable to authors, many businesses determine that the only form of intellectual property protection available to them is trademark protection. A retail clothing store may have no unique ideas or concepts, and, thus, it would not seek trade secret or patent protection. It would, however, seek trademark protection of the store's name. Its name should be unique and should enable it to stand apart from its competitors. Because of the limitations of trade secrets and patents, even a business with a unique concept may have no protection beyond trademark law. The first restaurant to offer drive-through service had a unique and valuable new concept. It could be kept a trade secret until launching, but once the first location opened, there was no way to keep the concept from being revealed to its competitors. Thus, trade secret law offered only a temporary solution. Drive-through service did not qualify for patent protection because it is not a process, machine, manufacture, or composition of matter. The best the restaurant could do was to establish a strong brand name that is protected under trademark law. Competitors could copy the drive-through concept but could not use a name that is confusingly similar to the original drive-through restaurant.

As an author, your work's value likely lies in your words. You may be writing about something that many before you have written about; perhaps a love story. In that case, your concept may not be unique. The value of your work lies completely in the words that you choose. In this case, your protection comes entirely from the copyright laws. On the other hand, maybe the subject you are writing about is unique. Perhaps you are a journalist and your investigation has led to solving a historic crime. You may be a scientist and you are working on a book about your scientific discovery. If you are an engineer, you may have designed a solution to a problem that has perplexed others in your field. In each of these instances, what you are writing about is unique and has value. Copyright law will protect your words, but not your underlying discovery. You have three possible options with respect to what you are writing about: trade secret protection; patent protection; or no protection.

For authors, trade secret protection is typically only a temporary solution. By sharing the information on a need-to-know basis and using confidentiality agreements, you can protect the theme, theory, or concept that will be revealed in your writing, but only until you publish your work. Once you publish it, you reveal the concept and you rely solely on copyright law to protect your work. It is sometimes possible to write about a subject and keep certain aspects of it a trade secret. You may write a series of articles on using hypnosis to kick addictions without ever revealing how you hypnotize a patient. Your method of hypnosis, if it is unique and confidential, remains a trade secret even though you have written extensively about the benefits of hypnosis. In that case, copyright protects your writings and trade secret law continues to protect the confidential information that you did not reveal in your writings.

Patent protection, on the other hand, is not precluded by published writings on the subject. It is important that the patent application be filed before any public disclosure of the invention (including a process or method) because in the United States a patent must be filed within one year of public disclosure of the patented invention. In many countries, there is no grace period and the patent application must be filed before the public disclosure. A good plan then, is to file the patent application and then write your article, white paper, or book about the invention. The invention will be protected under patent laws and your writing about the invention will be protected by copyright laws.

It is also possible that even though you are writing about something unique, it has no protection of its own. When Einstein wrote about the theory of relativity, he had discovered a universal law that could not be patented. Einstein *discovered* the theory of relativity, he did not *invent* the theory of relativity. In that case, although there was great value in what he was writing about, the only available protection was copyright law to protect the words he used to describe it.

Intellectual Property Protection Is Tied to The Unique Nature of the Work

Since intellectual property is designed to protect unique works, it is important to understand each aspect of your work that is unique. In some cases, only your words are unique. Thousands of authors have written about falling in love, but your poem or your love story expresses it in a string of words never used before. In other cases, what you are writing about is also unique. Perhaps you are describing a unique process and method. Perhaps your idea is different from what others have written about.

If you re-write a poem that has been written before, you have created no intellectual property. If you write about a system or method that was designed by someone else, your intellectual property is the unique words that you used to describe the system or method but you have no ownership in the in the system or method that you're writing about.

Let's create a hypothetical author to demonstrate the interplay. Jack Meyers has been a teacher for twenty years. He teaches children who have been diagnosed with Attention Deficit Disorder and he has recently developed a unique teaching method that has been far more successful than conventional teaching. It is so powerful that no teacher who knew the method would ever go back to trying to teach a child with ADD in a conventional manner of teaching. He has the writing skills and the resources to write and publish a book about this teaching method. He also has the skills to teach this method to other teachers. What are Jack's options for protecting and commercializing his teaching method?

Jack's work is potentially protected by every area of intellectual property law. He may receive trademark protection that covers the name of the teaching method as long as he chooses a unique name and as long as all users of the name are licensed by Jack to use the name. If he writes a book, copyright will protect his expression of the teaching method. The method itself is potentially protected by trade secret law or patent law. Because he cannot both publicize the method and keep it secret, Jack must make a choice between relying on copyright protection or trade secret protection. He must also determine whether it is possible to keep the method secret and still commercialize it. If he cannot, he must determine whether he qualifies for the strict requirements of a patent. Because it takes a great deal of skill to make that determination, Jack will want to hire a patent attorney to explore whether patent protection is available to him.

As Jack's lawyer, the first thing I need to do is explore Jack's goals. What is important to Jack? It may be recognition, it may be revolutionizing how children with ADD are taught, or it may be earning a passive income from his intellectual property. While Jack may have all of these goals, prioritizing these goals will dictate Jack's course of action.

Let's say Jack tells me that his most important goals are to revolutionize this area of teaching and receive recognition for doing so. He is okay with making less money as long as he helps as many children as possible. My advice to Jack is to write a book about the method and widely promote and distribute the book. If Jack refers to the method in the book as the Meyers Method, the name might catch on and become the generic name of that type of teaching (the Meyers Method name is not a trademark in this example because anyone can use it). Jack will be compensated from sales of the book. Copyright law will protect his expression of the method-the words in his book. It will not protect the underlying method and anyone is free to teach the method with or without modifications and with or without purchasing the book. The likely result is that the Meyers Method will completely replace conventional methods of teaching children with ADD, even in public schools.

On the other hand, maybe Jack has been earning a teacher's salary for far too long and has decided that his most important goal is to maximize his compensation from the use of the method. Or maybe it is important to Jack that the method is strictly adhered to with no modifications. In those cases, Jack may want to establish an institute to teach the method to others and provide a certification program for those trained in the method. He would want to establish a trademark, or brand name (perhaps the Meyers Method) and strict protocols for how the teaching method is administered. If there are aspects of the method that can be kept confidential even when the method is taught to students, then those aspects would be subject to trade secret protection. If there are no aspects that can be protected by trade secret, then Jack must consider whether his method qualifies for a patent.

As a prerequisite to enrolling in the certification program, teachers would have to sign an agreement. Among other terms in the agreement, teachers would agree to keep any trade secrets confidential, to take periodic continuing classes, to strictly comply with the protocols, to refrain from competing with the Meyers Method Institute, and to pay the Meyers Method Institute a royalty on all revenue they earn from the use of the method. In other words, the teachers who attended the Meyers Method Institute would each be licensees of the intellectual property who had the right to use the trademark (Meyers Method), and the trade secrets, (the Meyers Method protocol), or the patent, in exchange for agreeing to, among other things, pay a royalty. Curriculum would be developed for use in the school, and that curriculum would be protected by copyright law.

If Jack decides to proceed in this manner, his method is likely to reach fewer children with ADD than if he widely publicized it through the distribution of a book. This may be the best way, however, to commercialize the intellectual property because Jack can maintain quality control over the way that the method is taught.

I created a flow chart to help in analyzing which areas of

intellectual property best protect your work. We'll call it the IP Choices Chart. The first decision to make when utilizing the IP Choices Chart is whether the value lies in your expression or in what you are writing about. Remember that intellectual property rights flow from originality. Value also flows from originality. Thus, to determine value, consider what you have done that is your own unique contribution. Are your words unique while the underlying concept written about is not? Or is the originality in what you are writing about? Sometimes there is originality in both the concept and the way you express it. If you have written a poem about a tree, the value is entirely in the expression of the idea. There is no underlying idea, method, or process in a poem about a tree that is worthy of protection. What is highly valuable is the string of words you chose to describe the beauty of the tree.

If you write a paper describing a food processing method that preserves foods without destroying the nutritional content, the value is in the underlying process. The expression of that process has very little value. If you are writing a fiction novel that you haven't yet made public, there may be value in your unique plot as well as there being value in the writing that you have completed up to that point. The value in the idea, however, is temporary in that the plot is a trade secret only until you release the book to the public. Once the trade secret is revealed, the plot loses any intellectual property protection because anyone can write a book with the same plot as long as they write it in their own words. The expression (the way you tell the story), on the other hand, remains protected and valuable.

IP Choices Chart

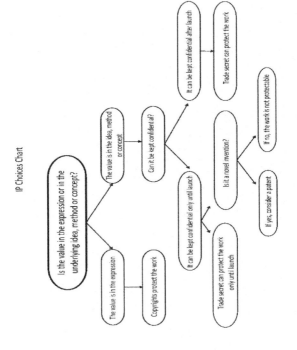

Is the value in the expression or in the underlying idea, method or concept?

- The value is in the idea, method or concept
  - Can it be kept confidential?
    - It can be kept confidential after launch
      - Trade secret can protect the work
    - It can be kept confidential only until launch
      - Trade secret can protect the work only until launch
      - Is it a novel invention?
        - If no, the work is not protectable
        - If yes, consider a patent
- The value is in the expression
  - Copyrights protect the work

Notice that the IP Choices Chart never mentions trademarks. Trademarks stand apart from other areas of intellectual property because they never protect substantial content. If you are writing about something, trademark never protects your writings and never protects the subject or concept about which you are writing. Trademarks may protect what you call it or how you present it. Trademarks protect brand names and brand identities.

Traditionally, trademarks were often the only intellectual property protection possessed by a business. If the IP Choices Chart leads you to determine that there is no copyright, trade secret, or patent protection to protect your work, it does not mean there is no value in your project. McDonald's® first launched the concept of a children's meal in its own bag with a toy. This brilliant idea was imitated by virtually every other fast food restaurant. Yet, McDonald's® continues to be incredibly successful in marketing to people with children. Part of that success has been through the sheer brilliance of the idea, and part has been great marketing coupled with a strong brand name or trademark. Many fast food restaurants have children's meals, but only McDonald's® has the Happy Meal®.

If you determine that you have a great idea that is not protected by copyright law, not protected by trade secret law, and not protected by patent law, what do you do? The answer is to do it anyway. Be the first to do it and be the best at it. Pick a unique trademark and build brand name recognition. Indeed, for the vast majority of Fortune 500 companies, their most valuable asset is the company's trademark. There are dozens of airlines around the world and they all provide essentially the same service. Southwest Airlines® built its success by providing stellar customer service. The trademark Southwest Airlines® is now synonymous with good customer service.

As authors, the IP Choices Chart will usually lead you to determine that the value in your work is in the expression and that the main protection that you need is under copyright law. Trade secret law will also be important to protect your work on a temporary basis until you publish your book. In some case, however, you may determine that what you are writing about is unique and valuable apart from your writings. Because you cannot publicize it and keep it confidential at the same time, you must determine whether there is potential patent protection or long-term trade secret protection *before* you publish the writing. Any trade secret protection is completely lost upon publication. Similarly, patent protection could be lost. In the United States, a patent must be filed within twelve months of when the invention is made public. In other countries, there is no grace period and patent protection is lost upon public disclosure. Thus, if you are writing about a unique process, method, or invention, you should consult with a patent attorney before you publish your writings.

CHAPTER 2
Understanding Copyrights and Copyright Ownership

What are Copyrights?

Copyrights are a bundle of legal rights belonging to the owner of an original work of authorship. Copyright protects "original works of authorship" that are fixed in a tangible form of expression. Original works of authorship simply means that there must be originality in the work. If you draw a check mark, there is likely no copyright protection in your drawing because there is no originality in a check mark. On the other hand, if you draw a dolphin, you have likely created a copyright-protected work.

The "fixed in a tangible form" requirement is best defined by the example of what is not fixed in a tangible form. If you give a presentation to an audience and the presentation is not written down, audio taped or videotaped, then it is not fixed in a tangible form. There is no copyright protection over the words that you used during that presentation because they are not preserved in any way. I often recommend to my clients that they record their presentations so that they do have a tangible form of the work.

The "fixed in a tangible form" requirement is not, however, a requirement that the work exists for any particular period of time. The work may be temporary. One of the most interesting questions I have been asked is whether a body painting is copyright protected. While the question is not directly answered by the statutes or the court cases interpreting the statutes, body painting is likely copyright protected because there is no requirement that the fixation last for any specific amount of time. Sand castles and ice sculptures are temporary art mediums that courts have determined are subject to copyright protection. These evanescent forms of artwork were fixed in a tangible form, if only for a very short period of time.

Copyrightable works include the following categories:

1. literary works;
2. musical works, including any accompanying words;
3. dramatic works, including any accompanying music;
4. pantomimes and choreographic works;
5. pictorial, graphic, and sculptural works;
6. motion pictures and other audiovisual works;
7. sound recordings;
8. architectural works.[4]

These categories should be viewed broadly. For example, computer programs and most "compilations" may be registered as "literary works" and maps and architectural plans may be registered as "pictorial, graphic, and sculptural works." [5]

There are several categories of materials that are generally not eligible for federal copyright protection. These include among others:

- Works that have not been fixed in a tangible form of expression;

- Titles, names, short phrases, and slogans; familiar symbols or designs; mere variations of typographic ornamentation, lettering, or coloring; mere listings of ingredients or contents;

- Ideas, procedures, methods, systems, processes, concepts, principles, discoveries, or devices, as distinguished from a description, explanation, or illustration;

- Works consisting entirely of information that is common property and containing no original authorship (for example: standard calendars, height and weight charts, tape measures and rulers, and lists or tables taken from public documents or other common sources).[6]

Section 102(b) of the copyright law provides that copyright protection does not extend to any idea, procedure, process, system, method of operation, concept, principle, or discovery, regardless of the form in which it is described, explained, illustrated, or embodied in such work.

It can be difficult to differentiate between the expression of the idea and the idea itself; which can make it difficult to determine what is and what is not a copyright infringement when using someone else's work as a source for your work.

One of my clients, Mary, had studied under and worked for Arthur, a well-known teacher, philosopher, motivator and author. He had created a body of work based upon seven principals of human nature. Mary had devoted more than ten years of her life to working with these seven principals and teaching Arthur's work to others. When Arthur passed away, the executor of his estate terminated all of Arthur's license agreements. Mary no longer had the rights to use Arthur's copyright protected work. Mary sought my advice as to whether she could write her own books and teaching materials based on the seven principals. Since ideas and concepts are not protected by copyright law, my answer was that she could use the concepts to write her own original works.

However, Mary had to be careful to create an original work and not copy Arthur's work. If Mary had sat down with Arthur's book in front of her and reworded each sentence or each paragraph, it could be considered copying. On the other hand, if Mary, without the aid of Arthur's book, simply wrote a new book using all of her own wording, it would not be copying even if it was based on the same seven concepts. It is important that Mary write the concepts themselves in her own words as well. She should not use Arthur's wording at all, including how he expressed the seven concepts.

Copyright law gives the owner of the copyright the exclusive right to do the following and to authorize others to do the following:

- To reproduce the work;
- To prepare derivative works based upon the work;
- To distribute copies of the work;
- To perform the work publicly; and
- To display the work publicly.[7]

The exclusive right to reproduce the work is the part of copyright law that is best known. We know that we cannot take an author's book and make reprints of it. The other rights belonging to the author of a copyright-protected work are less commonly understood.

Copyright law gives the author the exclusive right to make a derivative work based upon the work. This means that you need permission to write a play or screen play based on someone else's book because that would be a derivative work.

The author of an original work also has the exclusive right to distribute copies of the copyright protected work. This right is better described as the right to prevent the distribution of *unauthorized* copies. If you purchase fifty copies of this book from me, then you have the right to give or sell all of those copies to other people. Although you would be distributing the book, the "first sale" doctrine protects your activities. Under the first sale doctrine, a purchaser is permitted to resell or to give away a copyright-protected item that he or she purchased from the owner or an authorized distributor of the owner. Similarly, if you are the copyright owner and print 500 copies of your book, you retain the right to distribute those 500 prints even if you later sell your copyright to a publisher. On the other hand, if John Smith makes fifty unauthorized copies of a book and sells the unauthorized copies to you, your act of distributing the books would be copyright infringement.

Another lesser known protection provided by copyright law is the exclusive right to publicly perform or display the work. If Kim Jones decides to adapt your book into a play without your permission, she has made a derivative work in violation of your copyrights. If she then arranges for public performance of the play, she has violated your copyrights by publicly performing your work. If you originally wrote the work as a play, it is still copyright infringement for someone to publicly perform the play without your permission.

When do Copyrights Protect Works?

Copyright protection begins at the moment the work is fixed in a tangible form and ends upon the expiration of the applicable statutory period. Copyrights begin at the inception of the work regardless of whether the author has taken any steps to protect the work. There is a registration process, which provides valuable benefits, which will be discussed later. However, with or without formal registration, copyrights automatically protect the works.

Copyright Notices

Because copyright protection is automatic, you should include a copyright notice on your works, whether or not you have registered the copyright in the work. A copyright notice is not mandatory, but it is beneficial to put others on notice that you claim copyrights. As discussed later, the damages in a copyright case can be higher if the infringement is willful. If you use a proper copyright notice, it is difficult for the infringer to claim ignorance of your copyright protection. A proper copyright notice is © 2010, 2017 Jaburg & Wilk, P.C. The first year is the year of first publication, the second year is the year of publication of a revision, and the name is the name of the owner of the copyright.

When do Copyrights Expire?

Currently, in the United States, copyright protection expires 70 years after the death of the author or, if the work was created as a work for hire, 95 years from first publication or 120 years from creation, whichever is shorter. "Work for hire" is very specific and is described in more detail below. Once the copyright expires, the work becomes part of the public domain. As part of the public domain, the work can be used by anyone for any purpose and no longer enjoys any copyright protection.

Determining whether a work is in the public domain is tricky because there have been changes in the copyright laws, including in the duration of copyright protection. For any works created after the end of 1977, including works created today, the copyright protection lasts for seventy years beyond the author's death. However, to determine whether something created before 1978 is in the public domain is not as easy of a task. As a result of complicated statutes and changes in those statutes, we ended up with seemingly arbitrary copyright expiration dates. Any work that was neither published nor registered as of January 1, 1978, and whose author died before 1933 entered the public domain on January 1, 2003, unless it was published on or before December 31, 2002. If the author died in 1933 or later, the work will be protected for 70 years after the author's death, due to the passage of the Sonny Bono Copyright Term Extension Act in 1998. Unpublished works created as works for hire before 1898 are in the public domain.

If the work was published before 1923 and if it was first published in the United States, it is in the public domain. Works published from 1923 through 1977 are in the public domain if they were published without a copyright notice. Works published between 1978 and March of 1989 might be in the public domain depending on the publisher's compliance with notice and registration requirements that existed at that time.

Because of legislation passed in 1998, no new works will fall into the public domain until 2019, when works published in 1923 will expire. In 2020, works published in 1924 will expire, and so on. Copyright protection always expires at the end of the calendar year of the year it's set to expire. In other words, the last day of copyright protection for any work is December 31. For an excellent chart showing the date that works published after 1923 and works published abroad enter the public domain, visit https://copyright.cornell.edu/publicdomain. If that URL does not work, visit Cornell University's website and search the website for "public domain."

Who Owns the Copyrights?

Copyrights are generally owned by the creator of the work. While that seems to be completely logical, many people are very surprised to learn that the copyright is owned by the creator of the work *regardless* of who paid for the work. If you hire a cabinet maker to build and install cabinets in your house, you own the cabinets. It is understood that you have purchased the cabinets from the cabinet maker. Unlike tangible property, intellectual property cannot be transferred absent a written agreement. Thus, if you hire a ghost writer to write a book for you, the ghost writer owns the copyright. Absent a written agreement, ownership of the copyright is not transferred to you even though you paid in full. Indeed, you do not own the copyright even though you and the ghost writer may have a *verbal* agreement that you would own the copyright.

There is one exception to the rule that the creator owns the copyright of his original work. The one exception is a "work made for hire." The copyright law defines a "work made for hire" as:

> a work prepared by an employee within the scope of his or her employment; or
>
> a work specially ordered or commissioned for use as a contribution to a collective work, as a part of a motion picture or other audiovisual work, as a translation, as a supplementary work (a work prepared for a publication as a secondary adjunct to a work by another author for the purpose of introducing, concluding, illustrating, explaining, revising, commenting upon, or assisting in the use of the other work), as a compilation, as an instructional text (a literary, pictorial, or graphic work prepared for publication and with the purpose of use in systematic instructional activities), as a test, as answer material for a test, or as an atlas, *if the parties expressly agree in a written instrument* signed by them that the work shall be considered a work made for hire.[8]

The first type of work made for hire is a work made in the scope of an employment relationship. Be careful though; this does not include independent contractor relationships. For a work to be a "work made for hire" made by an employee, there must be a careful analysis of the nature of the relationship. To help determine who is an employee, the following factors that characterize an "employer-employee" relationship are considered:

1. Control by the employer over the work (for example, the employer controls how the work is done, has the work done at the employer's location, and provides equipment or other means to create the work);

2. Control by the employer over the employee (for example, the employer controls the employee's schedule in creating work, has the right to have the employee perform other assignments, determines the method of payment, and/or has the right to hire the employee's assistants);

3. Status and conduct of employer (for example, the employer is in business to produce such works, provides the employee with benefits, and/or withholds tax from the employee's payment.[9]

The closer an employment relationship comes to regular, salaried employment, the more likely it is that a work created within the scope of that employment would be a work made for hire.[10] At times, it will be difficult to determine whether the relationship will be considered by the courts to be an employment relationship. Thus, I recommend to my clients that they have a written agreement with employees who create content which governs the creation and ownership of any works protected by copyright law. The written agreement should reflect the intention of the parties, instead of relying on employment status to determine ownership.

The second type of work made for hire are the specially commissioned or ordered works that fall within one of these nine categories: (1) a contribution to a collective work (an article, column, or short story that has been published in a magazine, newspaper, or other periodical); (2) as a part of a motion picture or other audiovisual work; (3) as a translation; (4) as a supplementary work; (5) as a compilation; (6) as an instructional text; (7) as a test; (8) as answer material for a test; or (9) as an atlas. These categories are very specific and do not include the authorship of an entire book. If you are hiring someone to create a work within one of these nine categories, it may be a work made for hire, but the agreement *must be in writing*. The law does not recognize verbal work-made-for-hire agreements.

If the work is not a work made for hire because the author and the person hiring the author are not in an employment relationship and the work does not fall within one of the nine categories for specially commissioned work, then the author will own the copyright at the moment of creation. However, the author may transfer the copyright through a written assignment agreement. Copyrights cannot be assigned verbally so even a clearly stated intention and a handshake will not accomplish the transfer of the copyright.

If you hire someone to write something or to create any work covered by copyright law, such as an illustration for your book, you must enter into a written agreement in order for you to own the copyright to that work. Absent a written agreement that expressly states that you own the work, the law deems your usage of the materials to be a license rather than ownership. This is the most common mistake that I encounter in the copyright field. It is natural to assume that if you paid for it, then you own it. That is simply not the case!

Each of the following scenarios illustrates application of this concept:

- You hire a photographer to take your photograph for use on the cover of your book;

- You hire an illustrator to illustrate your book;

- You hire a graphic designer to create a cover for your book;

- You hire a translator to translate your book into another language;

- You hire a web developer to develop a website to market your book;

- You hire a copywriter to write marketing materials;

- You hire a videographer to produce a marketing video or a commercial to sell your book;

- You hire a screenplay writer to turn your book into a screenplay;

- You hire a film production company to turn your book into a motion picture.

In each of these cases, if you want to own the copyright on the work created by the person you hired, you must have a work for hire agreement (if the work falls within one of the nine categories) or a written agreement that assigns the copyright of the materials created by these third parties to you or to your company. Absent such an agreement, you are legally considered to be nothing more than a licensee of the materials created. The scope of that license will be determined by a court based on the oral and written communications that you and the author had leading up to the creation of the work.

You may be wondering whether it makes that much difference to own, rather than license, the copyright in someone else's creation that you paid for and are using. Ownership comes with the complete set of rights that every copyright owner enjoys. The right to copy, create derivative works, distribute, perform and display the work. One or more of those rights may be expressly or impliedly included in the license that you obtained; but without a clear written agreement you and the author may have a different perception of what you can and cannot do with the work. If you hire a ghost writer to write your autobiography and you do not get a written agreement, the ghost writer owns the copyrights to the manuscript and you are licensing them. There can be little dispute that your license includes the right to copy the manuscript since the whole point of what you paid for was to release the book on the market and sell copies. However, absent any discussion between you and the ghost writer, do you have the right to make derivative works? What if you want to substantially modify the manuscript and the ghost writer is opposed to doing so? As the owner of the copyright, the ghost writer may take the position that your license to use the work does not include the right to change it. What if you want to make a movie based on your book? Does your implied license with the ghost writer include the right to do so? If you had entered into a written agreement with the ghost writer assigning the copyright to you, it would be clear that you had the right to change the manuscript if you chose to do so and make derivative works from the book.

The importance of copyright ownership is also present when working with an illustrator. Perhaps your illustrator created a set of characters who are featured in your book. If at some point you decide to make plush toys based on the characters, you may or may not have the right to do so without your illustrator's permission. You certainly can if the illustrator assigned the copyrights to you or if you have a written license which permits you to do so. But absent anything in writing, it is unclear whether your implied license extends to the right to make plush toys.

You may ask what to do if you have already hired someone who has already created works for you and you mistakenly believed that you owned the works. Depending on your relationship, you might approach the creator and try to convince her to transfer the copyright of the work to you. This might require you to offer compensation beyond the compensation previously agreed to. If the author will not consent, and if you are not willing to move forward without ownership, you may be forced to hire a new independent contractor to create the work. If you decide to do that, it is very important that you not provide the new author with the work of the previous author. If your new illustrator sees the illustrations from the first illustrator, it greatly increases the chance that the new illustrator will be accused of copying them or creating a derivative work from them. If the new illustrator has never seen the first illustrations, they cannot copy them.

If the original author will not transfer the copyright, and if starting over does not seem like a feasible or financially sound option, you might negotiate with the original author for a license that meets your needs. The person you originally hired will likely be willing to work with you to spell out mutually acceptable terms of the license agreement. If you can work out license terms that are acceptable, then that may be a better option than completely re-creating the work. For example, if your illustrator is willing to put in writing that you have the right to use the illustrations in your book for as long as your book is published and that she cannot revoke that right, you might decide that is a better arrangement than hiring a new illustrator and starting over.

In summary, the following lists your options from best to worst if you find yourself in a situation where you do not own content that you paid a third person to create:

- Best case: the original creator assigns the copyright to you

- Acceptable (but expensive) alternative: you hire a new creator who creates a new work from scratch and assigns it to you

- Compromise: You and the original creator enter into a written license that permits you to do with the work everything your business plan contemplates

- Worst case: You have no written assignment and no license and a lack of clarity about whether your rights are broad enough to cover your business plan

Because it is so important to address copyright ownership and licensing issues in a clear and unambiguous manner, the next Chapter focuses entirely on that topic.

CHAPTER 3
Transfer or License of Copyrights

When the sole creator of a copyright protected work is the only person commercializing the work, then that creator has the entire "bundle of rights" related to the copyright in that work. The only licensee in that situation is the consumer who buys the book. Rarely is it that simple. More often than not, someone other than the author is commercializing the work. Sometimes, someone other than the author wants to own the copyright in the work. There are also times when there are two creators of a work. When someone other than the original creator is using a copyright-protected work, there has likely been a license of the copyright or a transfer of the copyright. It is very common for people to use the terms "sale," "transfer," "license," and "assignment" interchangeably or incorrectly. This can lead to ambiguity in written and verbal agreements and can result in the legal consequences of the arrangement being very different than what was intended by the parties.

There is a substantial difference between selling a product and selling the intellectual property rights related to that product. If you write a book and you "sell" me the book, you have simply sold me the tangible aspects of that copy of the book. You have not sold me your copyrights in the book. As the "owner" of the book, I have the right to read and enjoy the book and keep it on my bookshelf. I also have a "right of first sale," meaning that I can re-sell my copy of the book through an online marketplace, garage sale or a book shop or I can give my copy to my friend. I do not have the right to make additional copies of the book or to modify the words of the book. That is because I have purchased the tangible product, but I have not purchased the copyrights in the book.

When a consumer buys a single copy of a book, it is clear that there has been no sale or assignment of the copyright. On the other hand, the intention of the parties is often not clear when a company seeks the rights to commercialize your writings. The question is most often encountered when a writer writes an article for a newspaper, a magazine or other collective work. It also arises when a publisher seeks the right to publish your writings, or a producer seeks to make a play, television show or movie based on your writings. In those situations, the very first question you must ask yourself is whether you are assigning your copyrights to the other party or whether you are licensing your copyrights. The confusion is often created by the use of the words "sale" and "sell." Sale or sell implies the transfer or assignment of the item being sold. Yet, all too often, people enter into agreements that purport to "sell" rights, when the intention is to license the rights.

It is not unusual for a book to later be adapted into a screen play, a musical or a movie. When an author writes a book and then gives a third party the right to adapt it into a screenplay, this can often create confusion as to copyright ownership. It is common to hear writers say that they "sold" the movie rights or to hear producers say that they bought the movie rights. The sentence is internally inconsistent because if the producer only received the movie rights, then it was a license and not a sale. I can sell *all* of my copyrights, but I cannot sell a portion of my copyrights. If the only right the "buyer" has obtained is the right to make a movie from my work, then the "buyer" is really just a licensee and not a purchaser. The correct phrase is that you licensed the movie rights. If you really have "sold" the rights to the producer, then you have completely relinquished your copyright and the right to use or exercise any control over that work in the future.

A similar question arises if a publisher agrees to include your short story or article in its magazine. The first question you should ask yourself is whether you are selling (in other words assigning) the copyrights to the publisher or licensing the copyrights to the publisher. If you intend to sell the copyrights and the publisher intends to buy the copyrights, then there must be a clearly worded written agreement stating that you are assigning the copyright to the publisher of the magazine. If you do that, you no longer own the story, and you must get permission from the new owner to use it in the future.

Another common situation is when you have written a manuscript and a publisher seeks to publish the book. Established publishers have publishing agreements typically drafted by their attorneys and designed to protect the publisher. Occasionally, those agreements include a provision transferring the copyright to the publisher. Sometimes the agreements include rights to future books in the series or movie rights. It is essential that you seek the advice of your own attorney before entering into any significant financial agreement, including one with a publisher.

In the legal field, we often encounter poorly worded agreements that say that the author sold the story to the magazine, but also say that the magazine cannot modify the story or make a movie from it. The confusion is that a sale is the relinquishment of all rights and yet the author has purported to retain certain rights. It is inconsistent; if the magazine owns it, then the magazine has the right to do with it what it wants. If the magazine, on the other hand, has simply licensed the story, then the parties should not use the words "sale," "sell," or "assign."

It actually is possible to sell the copyright in something and also retain some rights. What is really happening in that situation is that you are assigning the copyright to the other person and that person is licensing certain rights back to you. Compare it to me selling you my boat and you agreeing that I can use the boat three times a year. You own the boat and you have title in your name. However, I gave you a discount on the price in exchange for you agreeing that I can use it occasionally. That is the equivalent of a sale with a license back to the seller.

The parties to an agreement can agree to an unlimited combination of terms. You can sell all rights, you can license some rights and retain others, and you can sell all rights and license back certain rights. The only thing you cannot do is sell *part* of your copyrights in a work.

As an author, you should always be aware of whether you are selling your copyright or licensing your copyright. In addition to all of the legal reasons to know the difference, the most practical reason is that it affects the price. If you are only licensing the rights to a story for the purpose of writing a screenplay and making a movie, the value of what you have given up is less than if you were selling all of your rights. If the publisher insists on owning the copyright to the story, then you should insist on being compensated for losing all of your rights to earn money on the story in other mediums.

While the amount of compensation is directly related to whether the deal is a license or a sale, the *type* of compensation is not. People often believe that the payment for a sale must be up front, while the payment for a license must be based on a percentage of sales and paid over time. That is often the case, but it is by no means a requirement. You can license your rights for a one-time, up-front fee if you and the other party agree to that compensation. Also, you can sell your copyrights to a third person and still earn a percentage of future sales. This type of arrangement is often seen with book illustrators. If you hire an illustrator to illustrate your book, you can ask the illustrator to assign ownership of the copyrights in the illustrations to you (which assignment must be in writing) and you may compensate the illustrator by an up-front payment, a percentage of book sales, or a combination. That compensation arrangement does not affect the ownership issue.

Co-Authorship Arrangements Create Special Challenges

Copyright assignments are often used to remove the uncertainty and risk associated with co-authorship. If two authors work together to author a book, they become joint owners in the copyright to the book. Unless the writing was separated in a determinable way, both authors own 50% of the whole. For example, if both authors contributed to every chapter and worked together to decide on wording, there is no way to differentiate between their work and no way to divide the copyright. On the other hand, if each author wrote certain chapters of the book and those chapters could be separated without destroying the work, then there might be a way to divide the copyright. Typically, that is not the case. Co-authorship can be problematic because if the authors have a disagreement, it can be as difficult as a child custody battle in a divorce. When co-authorship is contemplated, I often recommend that my clients enter into an assignment of the copyright to avoid joint ownership of the copyright. Either author can assign their rights to the other author in exchange for compensation, recognition, and other negotiated terms. If the co-authors cannot agree on one owner, they can form a company and assign the copyright to the company that they both own. The company, a limited liability company for example, should be governed by written agreements between the owners that address issues such as the death of one of the owners, divorce of one of the owners, buyout by one owner of the other's interest, and the procedure for dissolution of the company.

Chapter 4
Can I Protect the Title of My Book?

The most frequent question I am asked when I teach intellectual property to authors is whether the author can protect the title of his book. Unfortunately, book titles may be impossible to protect. The areas of intellectual property that are implicated are copyrights and trademarks.

Since copyrights protect the content of your book, one might think that copyright law also protects the title. It is, after all, part of the content. The problem is that copyright law only covers works that have enough originality to be protected. One-line phrases and quotes do not enjoy the protection of copyright law. You might argue that the book as a whole is a creative work and the title is a part of the book. Well, that is true. However, under the fair use doctrine, if I use a very small portion of your book, such as a one-line quote, I probably have not infringed your copyright. Since the title is a tiny fraction of the whole book, it enjoys no protection when separated from the whole. Courts and the copyright office unanimously agree that copyright law does not protect book titles separate from the content of the book.

Trademark Law Protects the Title of a Series

There is, however, another area of intellectual property that must be considered. A word or phrase that indicates a source of a product is a trademark and is entitled to protection under trademark law. The question then becomes whether the title of the book indicates its source. The answer is that the title of a single creative work does not indicate the source and is not protected under trademark law. The title of a series (two or more) of creative works can, however, be a trademark because once there is a series; the common title does indicate the source. The most common examples of book titles that enjoy trademark protection are Chicken Soup for the Soul® and the For Dummies® series.

If you plan on writing two or more books that are connected to one another, give them a common title, with each book in the series having its own separate sub-title. By doing so, you will create trademark rights over the common title.

The name of your book series is entitled to common law trademark protection based on your exclusive use. No registration is necessary to create common law rights. However, by registering a trademark with the United States Patent & Trademark Office, you are considered to be constructively using that trademark throughout the United States. It is usually a good idea to register the title of your book series with the United States Patent & Trademark Office in order to get that nationwide protection and other rights that come along with federal registration. While electronic filing of your trademark application is available to the public, the process can be tricky. It is wise to enlist the help of an attorney in filing for the trademark registration.

Because book series titles can be trademarks, and because books are related to other services and product names that have trademark protection, you should consider the trademark rights of others before choosing a title for your book. It would have been a bad idea for me to entitle this book Chicken Soup for the Author's Soul. That would very likely have invited a cease and desist letter and perhaps even a lawsuit against me. That is because reasonable consumers would likely be confused into believing that my book was published by or endorsed by the publishers of the Chicken Soup Series. Before settling on a title for your book, you should perform several searches. First, use internet search engines to determine whether your prospective title is being used and, if so, how it is being used. If you find a series of books with that title, you will want to go back to the drawing board and find a new name. Also, if you find related products, such as seminars or a movie, using that name or a similar name, you probably want to avoid that title. After your internet search, you can also search the United States Patent & Trademark Office at www.uspto.gov. At that website, you can search your proposed title. If your preliminary searches uncover no results, then your final step is to hire a lawyer or a trademark search company to do a professional search. This step is important. I always advise my clients to do their own searches first; yet I often find conflicts that are serious enough to warrant not using the proposed trademark.

Trade Dress

There is another aspect of trademark law that you should consider if you are writing a series of books: trade dress.

Visualize the cover of the For Dummies® series of books. [11] Every book in the series has a black and yellow color scheme so that us readers recognize the book as part of the series. The publisher of the For Dummies series has used that color scheme for so long that consumers easily recognize the book even without seeing the title.

This type of trademark is known as trade dress. Trade dress is the look of the label. If you have a single book with a great book cover, you have copyright protection over the design of that cover. If you have a series of books with a common cover design, you have both copyright protection and you may have trademark protection over that cover design. Once you have been using it long enough for consumers to recognize it, it is considered trade dress because it has acquired what is known as "secondary meaning" or "acquired distinctiveness." In other words, even before reading the actual title, the consumer recognizes the book as being part of the series because of its distinctive cover design.

While the bad news is that you cannot protect the title of a single creative work, the good news is that you can protect both the title and the cover design of a series of books that share a common title or a common cover design.

Fair Use

Another question that I have been asked is whether an author or publisher can use a trademark from an unrelated field as part of a book title. For instance, you may want to write a fiction story about someone who works at Macy's® and call it The Macy's® Man. This area of the law can be very fact specific, so you should consult with an attorney before moving forward with such a plan. While you have to be very careful to avoid any inference of affiliation or sponsorship by the trademark owner, your use *may* be acceptable under the trademark fair use doctrine.

Fair use of a trademark is use of a third party's trademark to describe that third party's product or service when your use does not imply sponsorship or affiliation. For example, if I have a Ford Mustang for sale, it is clearly fair use for me to place a classified advertisement or even a full-page ad offering the Ford Mustang for sale. I can use the Ford® and the Mustang® trademarks because I am describing Ford's product. If I build a custom car in my shop that resembles a Ford Mustang, it is not fair use to advertise that car for sale using the Ford trademarks.

But even when you are using someone's trademark to describe their product, it is still important to avoid any confusion. If the average consumer who encounters your use thinks that the trademark owner sponsored your work or that you are affiliated with the trademark owner, then you have infringed the trademark even if you are only using it to describe the owner's product. When you use a trademark within a book with proper references to the trademark owner, as I have done in this book, it doesn't imply sponsorship or affiliation. If you use the trademark in the title, it might imply sponsorship depending on the circumstances and disclaimers used.

In addition to an analysis of the fair use doctrine, your attorney will also consider whether your use can be considered to be defamatory or a commercial disparagement. If you intend to name names and reveal unfavorable information about a company's services or products, you must be prepared to back up your facts with evidence. I strongly recommend that you seek legal advice before venturing into this area. Using someone's trademark to disparage their product or service might be fair use of the trademark that is protected by free speech. On the other hand, without legal guidance, it is easy to cross the line from fair use to commercial disparagement of a trademark.

Chapter 5
Copyright Registration

Copyrights automatically attach to works in the covered categories that are fixed in a tangible form. Thus, when someone asks me to help them copyright their article or book, I always respond by saying that it is already copyright protected but they can strengthen that protection by *registering* the copyright.

Copyrights can be registered with the United States copyright office. There is no state level registration, as the federal government has sole jurisdiction over copyright issues. Federal law preempts (supersedes) state laws regarding copyrights.

The Importance of Registration

Although there is no requirement to register a copyright, the benefits of registration include:

- Registration establishes a public record of the copyright claim.

- Before an infringement suit may be filed in court, registration (or at least a pending application) is necessary for works of U. S. origin.[12]

- If made before or within five years of publication, registration will establish *prima facie* evidence in court of the validity of the copyright and of the facts stated in the certificate.

- If registration is made within three months after publication of the work or prior to an infringement of the work, statutory damages and attorney's fees will be available to the copyright owner in court actions. Otherwise, only an award of actual damages and profits is available to the copyright owner.

- Registration allows the owner of the copyright to record the registration with the U. S. Customs Service for protection against the importation of infringing copies. For additional information on customs protection, visit the U. S. Customs and Border Protection website at www.cbp.gov/xp/cgov/import and click on "Intellectual Property Rights."[13]

As of 2018, the copyright registration cost for electronic filing was $35 for an application for a single author, where the author is the same as the copyright claimant and it is for one work and the work is not a work for hire. All other applications cost $55. The process can take between three and seven months. There is a process for expediting a copyright registration. The Copyright office calls it "special handling" and charges an extra $760 to get the registration back to you in approximately one week.

The most important benefit of registration is its effect on recoverable damages. If you register your copyright within three months of publication or *before* an infringement occurs, you can recover your attorney fees from the infringer and "statutory" damages (a set range of money provided for in the statutes).

In a copyright infringement lawsuit, you can always seek what is known as injunctive relief – an order from the

Court that the infringer must stop selling the infringing products. You can also be awarded your actual damages. If the work is on the market, the sales history provides a basis for calculating actual damages. There are two possible ways to calculate your actual damages: (1) by your lost sales; or (2) by the infringer's revenue. These options are helpful if the work is being sold; whether by you or the infringer. Many times, though, there are no actual damages from copyright infringement, or the actual damages are dwarfed by the costs and attorney fees involved in filing a lawsuit.

Take, for example, a poet whose respectable poem ends up on a stranger's porn site. The poet has never registered her copyright in the poem. Also, the poet has not yet commercialized the poem and the porn site is not yet earning revenue from the website. The poet really wants her poem off of the website, so she visits me and asks me to handle the matter. I start by writing a strong demand letter to the owner of the website, but the website owner ignores the demand. Now, the poet wants to file a lawsuit. Remember that the poem needs to be registered before she starts the lawsuit. Thus, the poet must either wait three to six months or pay for special handling because she cannot file the lawsuit until the registration issues. That however, is the least of her problems. She has now found herself in the unenviable position of paying attorney fees in a lawsuit where she has very little damages to recover (remember no one has made any money off of the poem yet) and she *cannot* recover her attorney fees because she did not register the copyright before the infringement.

Let's revisit our poet's situation if she had registered the copyright on the poem before the infringement. First, she saves the $760 special handling fee. Next, she is entitled to statutory damages and to recover her attorney fees from the infringer. Remember that I said the infringer was earning no money off of that website. Our poet can be awarded: (1) an injunction ordering the website to take down the poem; (2) statutory damages of up to $150,000 for the willful infringement; and (3) her reasonable attorney fees expended in the lawsuit against the adult website. Most importantly, just having those remedies available to her greatly increases the chances that the website will voluntarily take down the poem without the poet expending substantial resources in a lawsuit.

When to Register

Clients often ask me when they should register the copyright on their work. The client's question relates to the stage of completion of the work. Yet, the answer is based, not on how far along you are with the completion of the work, but on whether you are disclosing the work. The right time to register is *before* you share the work with a third party who is not subject to a confidentiality agreement. Whether the work is still in outline form, in early draft, or completed, it need not be registered if you have not shared it with any third parties. On the other hand, regardless of the extent of completion, you should file for the registration before you submit it to a third party.

For example, if you have written a synopsis of your book and the chapter headings and then find yourself in a situation where you need to share that work with someone such as a potential investor, an illustrator, a coach, or a publisher, it may be time to register the copyright. You will have to judge your relationship with that third party and the level of trust. If you are comfortable that third party will not infringe your copyright, then you need not apply for registration at that time. On the other hand, if you do not have that comfort level, then filing the copyright at that time is a wise decision. Another option is to obtain a non-disclosure agreement from that third party. As illustrated earlier in the IP Choices Chart, whether to use a non-disclosure agreement or to rely on your copyright protection will depend on whether your goal is to protect what you have written or to protect the underlying concept. You can register the copyright to protect the portion that you have written and obtain a non-disclosure to protect any concepts or ideas that have not yet been included in the writing.

If you file for your copyright registration while you are still in the early stages of the writing, you will want to file again when you have added more content and need to share that additional content. You can submit the registration as many times and as often as you like, but you will pay the filing fee *each time*. One of the questions on the registration form is whether you have previously registered the work. You would simply answer that you have previously registered the work and explain that the reason for registering it again is that you have written more content.

The Registration Process

Not only is having a copyright registration a powerful tool in protecting your writings, it is surprisingly easy and inexpensive to obtain as the electronic filing fee is only $35 or $55. To encourage people to file electronically, the Copyright Office charges more if you do not register electronically. If you do not want to file electronically, for a slightly higher filing fee you can electronically fill in an on-line form that contains a bar code and mail the form to the copyright office by regular mail. The old fashion method of filling in a paper form by hand and mailing it in is also still available, but that is the most expensive and inefficient method.

This section walks you through the copyright registration process for filing online. If you decide to submit your copyright by regular mail, the Copyright Office website includes instructions for that process.

Prepare Your Materials for Submission

Before you begin the registration process, you must identify the materials to be covered by the registration. If you have written a single poem, article, story, or book, you will submit that work. You should submit the entire work. Thus, even if you have written a full novel, you must be prepared to submit the entire novel. If you submit a synopsis or an outline, then your copyright registration covers only that synopsis or outline and not the entire work.

If you have written multiple articles, multiple poems or multiple stories, you must decide whether you are filing a separate copyright registration for each one or whether you should combine them into a collection and register the collection.

If all of the following conditions are met, a work may be registered in unpublished form as a "collection," with one application form and one fee:

- The elements of the collection are assembled in an orderly form;

- The combined elements bear a single title identifying the collection as a whole;

- The copyright claimant in all the elements and in the collection as a whole is the same;

- All the elements are by the same author, or, if they are by different authors, at least one of the authors has contributed copyrightable authorship to each element.[14]

If your work is published, you can register the work exactly as you published the work. For example, if you distributed multiple copies of a poetry book that included fifteen of your poems, you can register the book with all fifteen poems. If you publish a book of short stories, you can register the copyright on the book. You can also register the copyright on the individual poems or stories if you choose to do so. Publishers of collective works that include works from many different sources can register the copyright over their compilation of the works.

Once you have identified the materials being registered, you must determine whether you can submit the materials electronically, or whether you must send hard copies of the materials to the copyright office. Even if you file electronically, you may need to submit materials by hard copy through the mail.

Textual works that are unpublished and textual works that have only been published electronically may be submitted to the copyright office as part of the electronic process. Works that have been published in hard copy may be *registered* via the electronic copyright registration system but you must *submit* the materials themselves in hard copy.

If you will be submitting your materials electronically, save the materials on your desktop or in an easily accessible file on your hard drive before you begin the process. The copyright office accepts a wide variety of file formats, and the following are most applicable to textual works like books:

.doc (Microsoft Word Document)
.docx (Microsoft Word Open XML Document)
.htm, .html (HyperText Markup Language)
.pdf (Portable Document Format)
.rtf (Rich Text Document)
.txt (Text File)
.wps (Microsoft Works Word Processor Document)
.fdr (Final Draft)

Filing For a Copyright Registration Online

Log on to www.copyright.gov, which is the copyright office's website. There you will find a great deal of information about copyrights for your perusal. I recommend reviewing the various circulars and reading the circulars that relate to any issues pertinent to you.

When you are ready to actually register your copyright, click on "Register a Copyright." You will need to create a new user profile before starting the process. After creating a profile, you may watch a tutorial about the electronic registration process or click on the prompt to start a new registration. After you complete the process of filling in the electronic application, the electronic system will prompt you to pay the fee and then upload the materials that you are depositing for registration.

Since you can save the electronic form at any time during the process, you do not need to complete it all at once. The next time you sign in, the system will give you the opportunity to return to the partially completed form.

The first step after signing in is to choose which form to use. In the left column, under the title "Register a Work," you will choose either the standard application (which has a $55 fee) or the application for one work by one author (which has a $35 fee). To use the less expensive form, you must be registering your own work in your own individual name with no other authors or illustrators.

Once you choose the form, you will click on "start registration" and then choose literary as the type of work. Between each section of the application, you will click "continue" at the top to advance to the next section.

Most of the questions on the form are easy to answer. The following four sections of the copyright form, however, may be confusing or require a bit more knowledge about copyright law.

1. Has this Work Been Published?

One of the questions is, "Has this work been published?" The definition of "published" given by the copyright office is the distribution or offer to distribute multiple copies of the work to the public. Thus, if you have written a self-help brochure and have been distributing it to your clients, the brochure is considered published for purposes of the copyright registration form. Also, if you have offered to sell your work to a group of wholesalers, publication does take place if the purpose of the offer is further distribution.

There is an interesting question as to whether a website or other online material is considered to be "published" as that term is defined by the copyright office. Many people assume that it has been published because it is made available for a widespread audience. Indeed, posting something online is often referred to as online publishing, even in the legal community. Yet, it does not satisfy the strict definition of publishing provided by the copyright office. If the online work is downloadable, however, such as an eBook, it is published because there is a distribution of multiple copies.

2. Who is the Author?

Another question on the copyright form that can be difficult is identifying the author of the work. If there is a single author who is also the copyright claimant, the question will be easy to answer. However, whenever there are multiple authors, authors and illustrators, or a company involved, this question will be more complicated. For example, if your book includes illustrations that were drawn by someone else, there are two authors of the completed book with text and illustrations. If the illustrator signed an *assignment* of his copyright to you, then you would list two authors: yourself with respect to the text and the illustrator with respect to the artwork. You would list only yourself as the copyright claimant. The form will prompt you to explain why the author and the copyright claimant are different and you will indicate that author of the illustrations assigned his copyrights to you by written assignment. On the other hand, if there has never been a writing that conveyed the copyrights to you, your options are to register only the text that you authored or to list two authors and two copyright claimants. If you choose the latter, you would essentially be registering the illustrator's copyright for the illustrator.

In determining who to list as the author, you also must appreciate the relationship between you and your employer or company, if any. As we covered earlier, an employer owns the copyright in works created by its employee in the scope of her employment. If you have formed a corporation or a limited liability company under which to write and publish your books, you will list your company as the copyright author if you were employed by your company when you created the work. In that situation, you will also answer yes to the question, "Is this contribution a work for hire?" If you were not an employee but you assigned the copyright to your company in writing, you will list yourself as the author and the company as the copyright claimant, and you will respond that it is not a work for hire.

In summary, apply these four rules in determining who to list as the author and claimant on the copyright form:

> Rule 1: The author is the creator unless the author was working under a work for hire (a written agreement or an employee in the scope of his employment).

Rule 2: The author is the employer if the work was created by an employee in the course and scope of his employment.

Rule 3: The author is the person identified as the author in a written work for hire agreement if the work falls within one of the following nine categories that can be a work for hire: for use as a contribution to a collective work; as a part of a motion picture or other audiovisual work; as a translation; as a supplementary work; as a compilation; as an instructional text; as a test; as answer material for a test; or as an atlas.

Rule 4: The copyright owner is the author unless there has been a written assignment assigning the copyright from the author to a third party or to a company.

3. Limitations on Claim

Another question that takes some analysis before answering is whether there are any limitations on the copyright claim. On this part of the form, you will indicate whether there is any portion of the work that you are submitting for which you are not claiming copyright coverage. For example, your book might be an interpretation or analysis of a Shakespeare play. Your book would likely include the play and your analysis and comment. When registering the book, you would indicate, by limiting the claim, that you do not claim copyright coverage of the play, which is in the public domain.

This is also the place in the form where you would indicate any portions of your submission that you do not own that are not in the public domain. As in our earlier example, if your illustrator never assigned the copyrights to you and your intent is to register the copyright on only the text of the work and not the artwork, you will indicate in this portion of the form that you are limiting your copyright claim to exclude the artwork.

Additionally, if you previously registered the copyright on this work and you are registering again because you have added new content, you will indicate that you are limiting your copyright claim to the new materials that were not previously registered.

4. Submission of the Work

After completing the form, you will be prompted to pay the filing fee. Your final step is then submission of the copy of the actual work. You will have the choice between uploading a copy and submitting it electronically with the registration form or printing a custom shipping slip generated by the copyright office that you will use to deposit hard copies of the work.

The method you choose is dependent in part on the mandatory deposit requirements of the Library of Congress, which is covered next. If you have never published the work, or have only published it electronically, the easiest and most efficient method is to upload the work in Portable Document Format (PDF) and submit it on-line with the copyright registration form.

Mandatory Deposit

Copyright registration is optional but depositing published works with the Library of Congress is mandatory. The Copyright Act establishes a mandatory deposit requirement for works published in the United States. In general, the owner of the copyright or the owner of the exclusive right of publication in the work has a legal obligation to deposit in the Copyright Office, within three months of publication in the United States, two copies for the use of the Library of Congress. Failure to make the deposit can result in fines and other penalties but does not affect copyright protection.

Before there was an electronic method of copyright filing, the mandatory deposit requirements were met by mailing two copies of the work being registered along with the copyright registration form. Because the copyright registration process is now electronic, while the Library of Congress still requires hard copies, there can be an extra step to properly deposit published works.

Federal law requires that the owner of a work that has been published in the United States must deposit two copies of the best edition of the work with the Library of Congress within three months of publication.[15] This mandatory deposit requirement applies whether or not you choose to register your copyright. If you choose to comply only with the mandatory deposit and do not want to register your copyright, you should send your deposit material to Library of Congress, Copyright Office-CAD 407, 101 Independence Avenue, SE, Washington, DC 20559-6607. Of course, it is hard to imagine any reason to forego copyright registration of a published work.

If you qualify for electronic deposit, you will submit your mandatory deposits in conjunction with your copyright registration. As the final steps in the electronic application, the on-line system will prompt you to state whether you will be uploading a digital file or sending a hard copy deposit by postal mail. The copyright office electronic registration system includes a notice about the restrictions of uploading a digital file. A digital upload alone will be sufficient if you have never published the work or if you have only published it online.

A digital upload will not be sufficient to satisfy the mandatory deposit if you have published a hard copy of your work. In that case, you will complete your copyright registration by printing a custom shipping slip generated by the Copyright Office during your electronic submission. The shipping slip contains information specific to your registration, so be sure to only use the shipping slip provided and to not use that same slip for any future submissions. Send the shipping slip along with your hard copies to the Library of Congress.

The Library of Congress requires deposit of the "best edition" of the work. When two or more editions of the same version of a work (hard and soft cover editions of books, for example) have been published before the date of deposit, the Library of Congress generally considers the one of the highest quality to be the best edition (the hard cover edition of a book, for example). If, on the date of deposit, a better edition exists but is not submitted, the Copyright Office is entitled to request the better edition on behalf of the Library of Congress. The Library of Congress lists the following criteria in judging the quality of printed materials for purposes of determining the best edition:

- Archival-quality rather than less-permanent paper

- Hard cover rather than soft cover

- Library binding rather than commercial binding

- Trade edition rather than book club edition

- Sewn rather than glue-only binding

- Sewn or glued rather than stapled or spiral-bound

- Stapled rather than spiral-bound or plastic-bound

- Bound rather than loose-leaf, except when you expect to issue future loose-leaf insertions. In the case of loose-leaf materials, this includes the submission of all binders and indexes when they are part of the unit as published and offered for sale or distribution. Additionally, the regular and timely receipt of all appropriate loose-leaf updates, supplements, and releases including supplemental binders issued to handle these expanded versions, is part of the requirement to properly maintain these publications.

- Slip-cased rather than not slip-cased

- With protective folders rather than without (for broadsides)

- Rolled rather than folded (for broadsides)

- With protective coatings rather than without

(except broadsides, which should not be coated)[16]

Under certain circumstances, special relief from deposit requirements may be granted by the Library of Congress. Requests are most often based on undue cost or burden to the copyright owner. Special relief is rarely needed for textual works because it is rarely expensive or unduly burdensome to deposit textual works.

Chapter 6
Getting Permission, Giving Attribution and Fair Use

We've covered the various laws and concepts you need to know to protect your work from infringement *by* others, but one important aspect of protecting your work is to be sure that it does not infringe the rights *of* others. Voltaire said "Originality is nothing by judicious imitation. The most original writers borrowed one from another." It is hard to argue against the proposition that virtually everything we write is based on something that has been written by someone else. Yet plagiarism is wrong and copyright infringement is illegal.

There is no clear line between basing your writings on someone else's work, which is perfectly acceptable, and infringement. While I can provide you some very helpful guidelines, my legal "disclaimer" is that if you ask two of the best intellectual property lawyers in the country to determine whether something is or is not copyright infringement, you will often get two different answers. The determination is fact specific and there are very few black and white rules.

The Difference Between Copyright Infringement and Plagiarism

Despite the common misconception that copyright infringement and plagiarism are the same, they actually have two distinct meanings. You infringe someone's copyright if you copy their work without permission, regardless of whether you give credit to the original author. You plagiarize when you fail to give credit to the original author and you pass the work off as your own, regardless of whether you had permission from the original author. Thus, it is both copyright infringement and plagiarism if I copy a chapter from someone else's book without permission and include it in my book without stating that I am not the original author of that particular chapter.

Unlike copyright infringement, plagiarism is not illegal. It is, of course, frowned upon. In the academic setting, most schools have strict rules against plagiarism and impose serious penalties. Journalists are bound by ethics rules that include a prohibition against plagiarism. Many organizations that govern authors have rules against plagiarism. Also, most publishers will prohibit plagiarism in their publishing contracts.

Idea Versus Expression

When determining whether you may be infringing someone else's rights, you must first consider the difference between copying the idea and copying the expression of the idea. The copyright laws do not prohibit copying someone else's idea. They do, however, prohibit copying the expression of the idea. The copyright statute states: "In no case does copyright protection for an original work of authorship extend to any idea, procedure, process, system, method of operation, concept, principle, or discovery, regardless of the form in which it is described, explained, illustrated, or embodied in such work."[17]

At what point then, does one cross the line between copying the idea and copying the expression of the idea?

Often, it is fairly easy to tell the difference. If I read or hear a presentation on how to make a gingerbread house and I go home and build a gingerbread house using what I have learned, I clearly have not infringed the presenter's copyright. Also, if I write my own instruction manual on how to build a gingerbread house, it will not be a copyright infringement as long as I use my own words to describe the process. On the other hand, if I copy the wording I read or heard in the presentation, I have crossed the line into copyright infringement.

To help shield yourself from accusations that you have infringed a copyright, always write something in your own words and without reference to any other materials. I call this "writing from scratch" because it is analogous to baking a cake from scratch rather than opening a box of cake mix.

Fair Use

Fair use in copyright law is a defense to copyright infringement. The Copyright Act provides that:

> ...the fair use of a copyrighted work...for purposes such as criticism, comment, news reporting, teaching (including multiple copies for classroom use), scholarship, or research, is not an infringement of copyright. In determining whether the use made of a work in any particular case is a fair use the factors to be considered shall include —
>
> (1) the purpose and character of the use, including whether such use is of a

commercial nature or is for nonprofit educational purposes;

(2) the nature of the copyrighted work;

(3) the amount and substantiality of the portion used in relation to the copyrighted work as a whole; and

(4) the effect of the use upon the potential market for or value of the copyrighted work.

The fact that a work is unpublished shall not itself bar a finding of fair use if such finding is made upon consideration of all the above factors.[18]

Fair use is a tricky concept because its application involves a subjective analysis. Many lawsuits have revolved around a use that one party believed was fair use of a work and the other felt was infringement. If you plan on using a work in a manner that you believe is fair use, you might consider seeking legal advice unless you are quite certain that your use is a fair use. Although permission to use a work is not required if the use is fair use, you might decide to obtain permission rather than risk a copyright infringement claim should the author disagree that your use is a fair use. If you are wrong about your use being fair use, you could be subjecting yourself or your company to a claim for damages, a court order enjoining your sale of the product containing the infringing content, and substantial attorney fees. For example, if you use a copyright-protected photograph in your book without permission, and your use is not fair use, the owner of that photograph could succeed in forcing you to take the book completely off the market until the book is reprinted without the photograph.

The most common fair use question I encounter is whether you need permission to use a quote or a line from a song. My writing coach loves the book called Quotationary, which is a compilation of famous, and not so famous, quotes. She once asked an employee of the publisher of Quotationary if she could use one of the quotes from Quotationary in her book. The employee responded that she could not use the quote. This response is surprising for two reasons. First, the use of a short one-sentence quote typically falls within the criteria for fair use. Second, and perhaps more importantly, the owner of the copyright in Quotationary does not own the copyright to the individual quotes. It owns the compilation of the quotes.

Whether or not quoting a line from song lyrics is fair use is a more difficult question. Like poems, songs are highly creative and can be fairly short. The copyright owner of a song may take the position that even a single line from his song is not fair use. Here again, the law does not provide clear guidance, only general guidelines. If you have any doubt, be conservative and get permission from the copyright owner.

A common myth is that a use is fair use if it is an internal use and is not distributed to third parties. For example, you might be tempted to copy an entire chapter of this book and provide it, free of charge, to others working with you. Your rational may be that you have not sold or distributed the copy outside of your own employees. The fair use test, however, gives great weight to the effect that your copying has on the owner of the copyright. A court is likely to determine that copying an entire chapter, even for internal use, is not fair use because you deprived the copyright owner of the ability to sell you multiple copies of the book.

A famous case that well illustrates this concept was a lawsuit filed by a group of publishers against Texaco. Texaco would subscribe to certain trade journals and circulate the journal to its researchers. There is no prohibition against circulating a single copy around an office or establishment. The Texaco researchers, however, would sometimes copy articles from trade journals that were of interest to them to keep it in their research files for future reference. The publishers took the position that Texaco was depriving them of the opportunity to sell Texaco multiple subscriptions. Texaco's position was that the copies were internal and for archive purposes of the individual researchers and, thus, the copying was fair use. The lower court and the appellate court determined that Texaco's use was not fair use.[19]

Most often, a fair use defense will succeed where the purpose of using the work is to comment upon it, criticize it, or parody it. A classic fair use would be if you write a magazine article reviewing a book and quote from the book in order to comment on the passage.

Getting Permission

Unless you have good reason to believe that a particular work is not copyright protected (such as it was first published before 1923), you will want to obtain permission to use the work. You may want to use a third party's textual passages, photographs, artwork, or lyrics. Leave yourself some lead time for obtaining permission since you will have to locate the creator and wait for a response. Do not wait until you are ready to publish your work.

Although a verbal agreement to use someone else's copyright-protected works is legally enforceable, you should always get your agreement in writing to avoid misunderstandings and disputes.

For more information about obtaining permission to use the works of others, the publisher Nolo offers a guide called *Getting Permission: How to License & Clear Copyrighted Materials Online and Off* by Attorney Richard Stim. The entire book, which is very well written, is dedicated to this topic. The book also includes relevant forms of permission letters, permission agreements, permission tracking forms and others.

It is important that your request for permission specifically identifies the materials that you seek permission to use and tells the owner how you will use the materials. Like most requests, you might want to tell the owner what's in it for them. If you are hoping to use the work without compensation, let them know how your use will benefit them, either through positive exposure or a boost to their sales. If you know that the owner will expect compensation, mention that you are willing to pay a fair price for the use. To learn the "going rates" for use of materials, research the clearing houses mentioned in the next section to see what they are charging for similar uses.

Determining Ownership

In order to get permission, you must first figure out who has the legal right to give you permission. There are several ways to determine who owns a particular work. First, if it is a published piece, look at the copyright notice. The copyright notice should include the year it was first published and the name of the copyright owner. If the work does not contain a copyright notice, it will be more difficult to determine the ownership.

The Copyright Office is also a great resource for determining ownership. The Copyright Office database is searchable online at www.copyright.gov. Although this is an excellent resource, keep in mind that because registration is not mandatory, the records will not be a complete listing of all copyright protected works.

If you are seeking to quote from a textual work, and if the work is published, you should first contact the publisher. The publisher may not be the copyright owner, but it has publishing rights that may include the right to give permission to use the work. It is often easier to find the publisher than it is to find the author.

There are also clearing houses that act as brokers for licensing works. These clearing houses can be a great resource because you can obtain permission for a large selection of works and because they are set up to automate the licensing process. For textual works, the Copyright Clearance Center at copyright.com is an excellent resource. The Copyright Clearance Center states on its website that it represents tens of thousands of authors and publishers and that it licenses the rights to millions of books, journals, newspapers, websites, eBooks, images, and blogs. Its website it fully searchable; allowing you to simply type the title you are looking for into a search box. For photographs, you may obtain permission from a stock photography agency, such as Getty Images or Corbis. If you run a search engine search for stock photography, you will find a plethora of resources. If you would like to quote music lyrics, BMI, ASCAP, and SESAC offer licenses.

As you are searching for the owner of the materials that you would like to use, keep a journal or a log of your efforts. If you are unable to find the owner and are still determined to use the work, your journal will help to establish your good faith efforts. If you ultimately decide to use the work without permission, consider the risk both in terms of the likelihood that the owner will make a claim against you and the most likely outcome of such a claim. For example, if you are using a small portion of the work, consider whether you have an argument that your use is fair use.

Complying with Copyright Laws

While it is easy to be careless about the use of third party works, it can be dangerous. The copyright laws provide for strict liability – meaning that there is no need for a copyright owner to prove that you intended to violate the law. Likewise, an innocent mistake as to whether something is in the public domain or protected by copyright laws is not a defense to a copyright infringement claim. The law provides copyright owners with powerful remedies that include the recovery of monetary damages and attorney fees and gives the courts the power to issue injunctions against the continued distribution of works that include infringing materials.

Willful copyright infringement is also a crime. While it is not common for law enforcement to pursue prosecution of those who infringe the copyrights of others, it does happen in more egregious cases.

In addition to the legal reasons to avoid infringing the copyright of a third party, there is the moral aspect. As authors, you understand the value of your intellectual property. Yet, people tend to be so much more tolerant of the theft of intellectual property than of tangible property. We teach our children to not shoplift, but many of us turn a blind eye when our children illegally download a song off of the internet. I always tell those who attend my workshops that you wouldn't borrow a stranger's car without permission, even if the owner was out of town and you returned it in the same condition you found it. You should be just as reluctant to buy one copy of a software program and make extra copies of it beyond what is permitted in the license.

Chapter 7
Public Domain and
Royalty-Free Works

Public Domain

It is not always illegal to copy existing works. Some works are in the public domain, meaning that they are not covered by any copyright protection. There are three ways that a written work can be in the public domain: (1) the copyright term has expired; (2) the author failed to follow a formality; or (3) it is a government-created work.

Duration of Copyrights

Determining whether the copyright on a work has expired can be difficult because of changes in the copyright laws. If you create a work today, the copyright will expire seventy years after your death. If the work was created under a work for hire agreement, the copyright will expire 95 years from the date of publication or 120 years from creation, whichever comes first. However, because of a major change in the law in 1978, that guideline is of little assistance in determining the copyright expiration date of a work created before 1978.

On January 1, 1978, the Copyright Act of 1976 went into effect. The Copyright Act of 1976 changed several basic features of the law. First, copyright protection became automatic for any work of authorship fixed in a tangible form and registration became optional. Second, it changed the term of copyright protection for new works to a period of the life of the author plus an additional 50 years after the author's death. Prior to this change, the term had been bifurcated. An initial term of protection was available for 28 years, and then a renewal term was available for another 28 years, but only upon application to the Copyright Office. In 1998, the term of a copyright was extended to a period of the life of the author plus 70 years.[20]

Because of the changes in the copyright laws, you cannot simply determine when the author died and count forward seventy years. That method will only work if the work was written after 1978. A great tool for determining whether a work has entered the public domain is provided by Cornell University at: https://copyright.cornell.edu/publicdomain. The University of North Carolina also provides a helpful table of dates at http://www.unc.edu/~unclng/public-d.htm. One very simple test is that all works published before 1923 were in the public domain as of January 1, 2009. Beginning in 2019, additional works will fall into the public domain on a rolling basis. If the work you are investigating was created between 1923 and 1978, consult either the Cornell University or the University of North Carolina chart for the copyright status of the work.

The Author or Publisher Failed to Follow a Formality

Although placing a copyright notice on your work is not mandatory, it is a good idea. At one time, using a copyright notice on a published work was mandatory, and failure to do so resulted in the loss of copyright protection and the work entering the public domain. Specifically, works published between 1923 and 1977 are in the public domain if they were published without a copyright notice. Works published in 1978 through 1989 without the copyright notice and without subsequent registration within five years are also in the public domain. Another statutory formality that existed at one time was copyright renewal. Works that were published from 1923 to 1963 even with notice are in the public domain if the registrant did not renew the copyright registration.

The Cornell University and University of North Carolina charts also do a nice job of illustrating how failure to follow formalities affects copyright status.

Government Works

You may have noticed that in this book, I have extensively quoted from works of the United States government, specifically the Copyright Office. Although giving proper credit is still important to avoid plagiarism, there was no need for me to obtain permission from the government to use these quotes. The Copyright Act provides, "copyright protection under this title is not available for any work of the United States Government, but the United States Government is not precluded from receiving and holding copyrights transferred to it by assignment, bequest, or otherwise."[21] The Copyright Act defines government works as "a work prepared by an officer or employee of the U.S. government as part of that person's official duties."[22]

While having the ability to use federal government works without permission is a great benefit, it is not without limitations. First, the rule applies only to works of the federal government, not to those of state and local governments. Also, some works of the federal government contain the works of others. For example, if you look up a patent, you might think that is a work of the federal government, since the government issues patents. However, the patent itself is a derivative of the patent application, which was likely written by an attorney. The wording of the patent is probably protected by copyright.

Another area of caution is distinguishing between works created by government employees and those written by government contractors. If it was created by a government employee, it will be public domain. If it was created by someone under contract with the government, the contract itself will govern whether the works will be in the public domain. For example, NASA is under contract with the federal government. All of the photographs of space taken by the Hubble Telescope are in the public domain because NASA's contract with the government provides that their works are in the public domain.

How to Determine Public Domain Status

Thanks to the internet, it is not as difficult as it used to be to determine whether a particular creation is in the public domain. If you know when the work was published, you can often determine whether the work has passed into the public domain because of the expiration of the copyright. If you do not know the date of creation or publication, you may be able to determine it through research on the internet. There are also websites dedicated to listing all materials in the public domain. Project Gutenberg, at www.gutenberg.org has a comprehensive collection of public domain material.

If you are using a work that is in the public domain, make sure you are using the public domain version. Some works that pass into the public domain are the subject of derivative works by third parties. The third party may have copyrights to any original works of authorship that they contributed to the work. For example, a Shakespeare play is in the public domain, but a modern adaptation of it would not be. If you use the original play, you do not need permission. On the other hand, if you use a modern adaptation of the play, you would need permission.

The United States Postal Service was sued for using an image of the Statue of Liberty on a postal stamp. While the original image of the Statue of Liberty is in the public domain, the image on the postal stamp was actually an image of the reproduction of the Statue of Liberty built at New York, New York® casino in Las Vegas.

If you are unable to determine the status of a particular work, try to contact the creator of the work, or consult with an attorney experienced in intellectual property law.

Royalty-Free Works

Some works are not in the public domain, but the owners have dedicated them to public use without charge and without the need to seek permission.

Common forms of royalty-free works are clip art, templates, and works licensed under Creative Commons.

Clip Art and Templates

Clip art and templates are available for public use without the payment of a royalty. Clip art and templates are often misconstrued as material in the public domain. In reality, clip art and templates are usually copyright-protected, but the creators have made them available for royalty-free use. The distinction is important because there is no restriction on how you can use materials that are in the public domain. Materials such as clip art, however, are usually provided for use under license restrictions that can be found in the fine print agreement or terms and conditions of the clip art provider. For example, Microsoft Word includes a clip art library. The End User License Agreement for Microsoft Word provides that I may use the clip art and may modify the clip art but provides four limitations on my use: (1) I may not sell the clip art; (2) I may not license the clip art; (3) I may not use the clip art in a way that would imply sponsorship or endorsement by an agency or company; and (4) I may not use the clip art in a manner that is obscene or scandalous. Those are pretty reasonable limitations, but they are limitations. Some license agreements permit personal, but not commercial use of the clip art or the template. When using clip art or templates, it is important that you read and comply with the license agreement or the terms and conditions.

For example, on my advice, one of my clients approached his graphic designer to request that she assign to him the copyright in a logo that she created for his business. She responded that she was unsure if she could assign the copyright in the logo because she adapted the logo from a clip art graphic. In other words, she was not the original creator. We located the terms of use of the clip art and we learned that the terms prohibited use of the clip art in logos. Our research had revealed that not only could my client not own the copyright in his logo, but he was not even allowed to use it. He had to commission a new logo.

Creative Commons

There has been a growing trend of owners permitting their works to be used free of charge in furtherance of a common goal of improving the work through collaboration. Some people call it the "copyleft" movement. The driving force behind this movement is an organization called Creative Commons. Creative Commons is a non-profit organization that "works to increase the amount of creativity (cultural, educational, and scientific content) in "the commons" — the body of work that is available to the public for free and legal sharing, use, repurposing, and remixing."[23] Creative Commons has established four main types of licenses under which copyright owners can choose to publish their works: (1) attribution alone, in which the only obligation of the user is to give attribution; (2) noncommercial use only; (3) no derivative works allowed; and (4) sharealike, in which you may make derivative works as long as you similarly license any derivative works. There are also combinations of the four main types of licenses.

Perhaps the most popular user of the Creative Commons license structure is Wikipedia, which provides an attribution-sharealike license to its users. If you wish to use material that is under a Creative Commons license, look for these Creative Commons symbols which are used by the copyright owners to reflect which uses the owner permits:

 Attribution

 Sharealike

Noncommercial

No Derivative Works

Chapter 8
Based on a True Story

This chapter is different from every other chapter in this book in one important aspect: the concepts in this chapter may vary from state to state. Copyrights and trademarks are based on federal law, not state law. Trade secrets are governed by federal law and state law. The laws related to defamation, privacy rights and publicity rights, however, can be substantially different from state to state.

Because of the differences in state laws, it is particularly important that you seek legal advice if you plan to write a true story or a fictional story about a real person or company. An experienced defamation law attorney can perform a pre-publication review of your book or article to help identify areas of risk. This chapter covers general legal concepts in these areas but does not cover the nuances of each individual state.

Defamation

Let's face it, people do not like it when others tarnish their reputation. On the other hand, our country prides itself in the First Amendment and the right to free speech. Courts are often faced with the difficult challenge of balancing an author's right to free speech against the subject's right to protect her reputation. The balance will usually tip in favor of free speech unless your writing contains a false and disparaging statement of fact. In the United States, if the statement is true, it is not defamation even if it is a highly disparaging statement. Some other countries do not allow disparaging statements to be made, even if they are true.

A statement must also be a fact, not an opinion, to be defamatory. Stated another way, I have a right to express my opinion even if that opinion is disparaging of another person. It is not always easy to separate fact from opinion, and I have litigated numerous cases in which the deciding factor was whether the statement was one of fact or opinion. If I write an article that states that John Smith drinks a fifth of vodka every day, I have committed defamation if the statement is not true. If my article instead states that John Smith drinks too much, that is very likely an opinion because my idea of drinking too much could be having one drink per month. A more difficult question would be if I wrote that John Smith is a drunk. That is probably an opinion, but John Smith could argue that it is a false factual statement.

Legally, you cannot defame a deceased person because defamation is a personal claim that cannot be brought by the surviving family. Thus, you are far less likely to get sued for defamation if the object of your ridicule has passed on. Use caution, though, if your statements are directly about the deceased person, but have a negative impact on the reputation of someone who is still alive.

If you are considering writing a story or book that depicts or appears to depict a true story, then you should first consider whether your story will cast anyone in a false negative light. If it will, you should consider whether that person or the people involved are likely to file a claim against you. If so, seek legal advice before you publish your story. An attorney familiar with defamation law can review the book and help you to avoid making any false statements of fact. A review by an attorney can avoid a lawsuit such as the lawsuit that was filed in August of 2009 against the authors and publisher of "American Icon: The Fall of Roger Clemens and the Rise of Steroids in America's Pastime." The lawsuit was filed by Kelly Blair and alleges that the book falsely stated that Kelly Blair pushed steroids on major league baseball players. Perhaps the authors and publishers of the book never considered that Mr. Blair would not only dispute the assertion, but also would seek relief from the courts to clear his name.

It is sometimes difficult to know what types of statements will offend people enough to prompt them to turn to the courts. In September of 2008, Donald Trump sued the author of "TrumpNation: The Art of Being The Donald" because the author stated that Trump was worth $150 million to $250 million. Trump asserted in the lawsuit that he is worth billions of dollars and that the author hurt his reputation by understating his net worth. Anytime you are making factual statements about a real person, you must exercise the utmost of caution to avoid finding yourself as the defendant in a defamation case.

Invasion of Privacy

While a true statement of fact is never defamation, it could run afoul of state privacy laws. The right of privacy is invaded by the unreasonable intrusion upon the seclusion of another, unreasonable publicity given to the other's private life, or publicity that unreasonably places the other in a false light before the public.[24]

Someone who gives publicity to a matter concerning the private life of another is subject to liability to the other for invasion of his privacy, if the matter publicized is of a kind that (a) would be highly offensive to a reasonable person, and (b) is not of legitimate concern to the public.[25]

If my buddy Sue tells me that she is HIV positive, I cannot publish an article, a book, or a story about her ordeal. Sue has an expectation of privacy that was not waived merely because she confided in me. It would be unreasonable for me to publicize her plight without her permission. On the other hand, if Sue is a public figure, such as a celebrity, then her private life is likely to be considered to be of concern to the public. The question of whether she had an expectation of privacy when she confided in me would be a closer call if she is famous.

Because the determinations of whether the disclosure is reasonable, whether it would be highly offensive, and whether it is of legitimate concern are fact specific questions, it may be very difficult to predict whether your publication may subject you to liability. After factoring in the differences in the law from state to state, predicting the likelihood that you will get sued or prevail in a lawsuit may be as accurate as predicting a bet on the roulette wheel.

Publicity Rights

Publicity rights are implicated when a celebrity's name or likeness is used in a way that implies sponsorship or consent. I once had a client who was a competitive surfer. One day, he walked up to a vending machine to buy a soda and found himself looking at a picture of himself. The vending machine displayed an action shot of my client surfing a wave. While he was flattered, he was also keenly aware of the fact that no one sought his permission (or paid him a royalty) to use his likeness. Since his picture was being used in a commercial context to advertise a product, the use was a violation of his publicity rights.

Publicity rights were first recognized by courts in 1953 when a federal appellate court stated that a baseball player "has a right in the publicity value of his photograph." [26] The right of publicity has more recently been defined as the "inherent right of every human being to control the commercial use of his or her identity."[27]

Publicity rights may also be implicated if you use the image of someone who is not famous. It is a good idea to obtain a written release from the subject of a photograph if you are going to use the photograph in a manner that might be considered a commercial use, i.e. you are making money off of the use of the photograph. A release is a straight forward contract in which the subject of a photograph or other image gives up their right to sue you for using the image.

While some states have no laws regarding the use of someone else's likeness, other states have very strict laws. California, for instance, has one of the most comprehensive restrictions on the use of someone's likeness for commercial purposes. The California law provides:

> Any person who knowingly uses another's name, voice, signature, photograph, or

likeness, in any manner on or in products, merchandise, or goods, or for purposes of advertising or selling, or soliciting purchases of products, merchandise, goods or services, without such person's prior consent, or, in the case of a minor, the prior consent of his parent or legal guardian, shall be liable for any damages sustained by the person or persons injured as a result thereof. In addition, in any action brought under this section, the person who violated the section shall be liable to the injured party or parties in an amount equal to the greater of seven hundred fifty dollars ($750) or the actual damages suffered by him or her as a result of the unauthorized use, and any profits from the unauthorized use that are attributable to the use and are not taken into account in computing the actual damages. In establishing such profits, the injured party or parties are required to prove his or her deductible expenses. Punitive damages may also be awarded to the injured party or parties. The prevailing party in any action under this section shall also be entitled to attorney's fees and costs.[28]

California has a similarly-worded statute for deceased persons, which permits the heirs of the deceased person to bring the claim. The portion of the statute extending the rights to deceased persons was not enacted until 1984 and was a reaction to a California lawsuit brought by the heirs of Bela Lugosi who sued to stop Universal Studios from licensing Lugosi's Dracula on merchandise. The Court determined that someone's right to stop others from exploiting their likeness did not survive their death. The Court decision was, not surprisingly, met with protest by Hollywood celebrities and their families, leading to the California legislature expressly extending the rights beyond the death of the celebrity.

Since there is a variance among the state laws on this issue, the question arises as to which state's laws will apply. That question was recently answered by the California Court in a case related to photographs of Marilyn Monroe. In that case, the Court found that since Marilyn Monroe lived in New York at the time of her death, New York law must be applied to the issue. Since New York publicity rights do not survive the death of the celebrity, the California court determined that Marilyn Monroe's right to publicity did not survive her death.

Publicity rights, however, will not prevent you from writing a story or article about a famous person. The laws attempt to balance the rights of publicity against the First Amendment rights of authors. When another person's identity is used in a book or article, the courts generally consider the use as expressive or non-commercial and protected by the First Amendment.

Famous people enjoy less privacy because events in their lives are considered to be of public interest. The story, however, must be written in such a way that there is no inference or implication of sponsorship or permission by the famous person. It may also be a good idea to include a disclaimer that states that the contents have not been endorsed, reviewed or confirmed by the celebrity.

Trademark Infringement/ Trade Disparagement

Like individuals, companies can be sensitive about protecting their brand names and their reputations. If you are considering referring to a company or product name in your writings, you must first analyze whether your use may be considered trademark infringement or trade disparagement.

Use of a trademark in your writings in a manner that does not imply sponsorship or affiliation is likely permissible as nominative fair use of the trademark. Usage of someone else's trademark to describe the trademark owner's product is nominative fair use as long as the product or service cannot be readily identified without using the trademark, the user only uses so much of the mark as is necessary for the identification, and the user does nothing to suggest sponsorship or endorsement by the trademark holder.[29] I may decide to write a book or a short story about my first car, a 1970 red Ford® Torino GT convertible. There is no need for me to describe the car as a convertible made by a popular American car maker. I can simply write that it was a Ford. I cannot, however, use the Ford trademark or emblem in a manner that might confuse the reader into believing that Ford has endorsed or sponsored my statements. I also should include the ® registered symbol next to the trademark and a statement that "the trademarks referred to in this book are the property of their respective owners."

If I am writing an article or a book that might infer sponsorship, I would include a clear disclaimer. For example, if I wanted to write a manual entitled *The Complete Guide to the Ford Torino*, I should be very careful to make it very clear that I have no affiliation with Ford and that Ford has not sponsored the guide in any way. The most conservative approach would be to obtain permission from Ford.

My experience with my first car was nothing but positive. Had it been otherwise, I might contemplate writing a story about the unreliability or danger of my car. That might be a good time to use a fictitious manufacturer instead of a real trademark. For example, if I am writing an autobiography and part of that autobiography concerns the mechanical failure of my car leading to my serious injury, I might not want to reveal the manufacturer's name. This, of course, depends in large part on your tolerance for risk. You may be writing your story *because* you want the public to know the dangers or risks of a certain product. In that case, using a fictitious name would defeat the purpose.

If your goal is to create a work that reveals something negative about a product or service, I strongly urge you to seek legal advice from an attorney well-qualified in the field. The attorney will help you decrease the chance of a lawsuit or increase your chance of success in the event of a lawsuit. When Morgan Spurlock made the movie *Super Size Me,* he consulted with legal counsel. Indeed, the movie credits list four attorneys as legal consultants. Mr. Spurlock was careful to only make statements that he knew he could prove were true. He took a calculated risk in order to disseminate his message about the health risks of eating too much fast food.

Chapter 9
International Rights

A successful book is often sold abroad and translated into other languages. The popularity of ecommerce transactions and eBooks makes it more likely than ever that a writing created and published in the United States will make its way to other countries. The global nature of today's commercial transactions raises the question, "What protection is available for my book outside of the country?"

Trademarks

Trademark rights are limited to the country of use and registration. If you register your trademark with the United States Patent & Trademark Office, your rights and benefits do not extend into foreign countries.

As discussed earlier, if you have a book series with a common title, you may have trademark rights in that title. If you register your trademark, it extends your trademark rights to the entire United States, but not beyond. Thus, if you plan on selling your series abroad, you will want to protect your trademark in the countries in which you are selling the books. There is no such thing as an international trademark. Each country has its own laws and its own registration system. The only trademark registration that covers multiple countries is a European Union trademark which will cover all of the countries that are members of the European Union.

There are two methods for registering a foreign trademark. You can have your local trademark attorney work with foreign counsel to obtain the registration or you can have your local trademark attorney register the trademark through the Madrid Protocol. The Madrid Protocol is a system wherein a foreign trademark is filed through the United States Patent & Trademark Office. In order to utilize the Madrid Protocol, the country in which you are seeking registration must be a signatory to the treaty. You can find a list of participating countries at www.wipo.org. Filing a registration using the Madrid Protocol is not necessarily the better option. The application is still subject to review by the foreign country and if there are objections, you may still need to hire a local attorney in that foreign country. Also, because the Madrid Protocol application is tied to your United States application, there is a risk that you could lose your foreign application if something goes wrong with your United States application.

If you decide to skip the Madrid Protocol and file directly with the foreign country, you still may want to seek assistance from your local trademark attorney. It can be intimidating locating and hiring attorneys in foreign countries. Ask your local attorney if he is a member of INTA, which is the International Trademark Association. INTA members are part of an international network that helps to identify and secure foreign counsel.

Copyrights

Unlike trademark laws, copyright laws do extend beyond country borders. The United States is a signatory to the Berne Convention for the Protection of Artistic and Literary Works, an international treaty that provides that, "Authors shall enjoy, in respect of works for which they are protected under this Convention, in countries of the Union other than the country of origin, the rights which their respective laws do now or may hereafter grant to their nationals, as well as the rights specially granted by this Convention." Essentially, the Berne Convention provides that its member countries will honor the copyright laws of other member countries.

The Berne Convention was first adopted in 1886, but the United States did not become a member until 1989. There are 174 signatories to the Berne Convention, including all but the most obscure countries.

Under the Berne Convention, the minimum period of protection is fifty years after the author's death. Countries that are members can extend that time period but may not reduce it.

The laws of the country of first publication govern the copyrights of a work. Interesting and complex legal questions arise when a work is published in two different countries that have different copyright terms. For example, the copyrights for Sherlock Holmes stories expired in 1980 in Canada and in 2000 in the United Kingdom. In the United States, certain Sherlock Holmes works are still protected by copyrights laws but most are in the public domain.

Chapter 10
Online Works

For the most part, the laws that protect and govern writings are the same whether the work is distributed in traditional paper form or online. There are some practical differences in the way people treat the works that led Congress to pass the Digital Millennium Copyright Act.

As was discussed early in this book the copyright to a work is generally owned by the creator of the work. That is the case with digital or online works as well. It is very common to hire a third party to create a website for you or to write software code. Remember that just because you hire and pay them does not mean you own what they create. If you want to own the work, you must get a written agreement transferring ownership.

Website development is often a collaborative process. You may provide your web developer with text and photographs, there may be a third party graphic artist who does the layout and graphics, and there may be a developer who writes the code so that the website functions in an online environment. Absent a written agreement transferring ownership to you, the website as a whole will not be owned by any one person or entity. Rather, each creator owns what that owner created.

The practical problem arises when you want to change your website or move it to another host. I once had a client who found himself as the defendant in a copyright infringement lawsuit after he hired a web developer, paid the full amount requested by the developer for the website and then later moved the site to a new host. The web developer took the position that as the owner of the copyright (which he was) he did not give my client permission to have the site hosted by another company. Had my client known that he needed a written agreement that included a provision transferring the copyright to him, he could have avoided that dispute and saved substantial attorney fees. While it is unusual that this situation would result in a lawsuit, it is actually a common disagreement.

Unfortunately, the solution may not be as simple as having the developer assign the copyrights to you. First, your website may be based on a template. One of the most inexpensive ways to obtain a website is to use a template driven model. In that case, the provider of the templates is not going to agree to transfer the copyright to you. Depending on the price, you might have to be satisfied with a written agreement that clearly sets forth the extent of your usage rights. This may be an issue even with a custom-built website. Most developers have a core program that they use as a basic foundation that they customize. Once again, you may need to be satisfied with a license to use that core program. The key is to be sure the license permits you to move your website to a new host and make changes and updates to your website as needed for your business.

Substantively, copyright and trademark protection are the same in the digital world and on the internet as in traditional form. Many people mistakenly believe that when a work is available on the internet, it is in the public domain. Remember that public domain means that the work is not protected by copyright laws. Posting a work on the internet does not remove or even change the work's copyright protection.

The only practical difference is the likelihood that the copyright will be infringed. Works available in cyber space are more likely to be the subject of unauthorized copying. This may be the result of people's misconception about copyright protection over online works, it may be because the online work is more accessible and easier to copy than its paper counterpart, or it may be a combination of these factors.

Because copying of online works is rampant, it is a good idea to take both legal and technological precautions to protect your online works.

One precautionary measure that you may want to take is to use a plain language warning in addition to the copyright notice. Because some unauthorized copying really is the result of ignorance, you can reduce the likelihood of infringement by educating your reader. Use a traditional copyright notice but add a sentence similar to the following: "This article is protected by the copyright laws of the United States as well as international treaties. Do not copy this article without written permission from [fill in the copyright owner's name]." Alternatively, if you do not mind the article being copied, you might state, "This article is protected by the copyright laws of the United States as well as international treaties. You may copy this article without permission from [fill in the copyright owner's name] but you must give credit and you may not make any modifications to this article."

If your work will appear online, it is particularly important that you register the copyright with the

United States Copyright Office. You also should keep the registration up to date. It is easy to add additional materials to online works. For example, most websites are updated on a regular basis. When new content is added the website after the registration is filed, that new content is not automatically added to the copyright registration. Rather, a new registration must be filed which indicates that it covers the new materials.

If your work is very valuable, or if you have a particular concern about copyright infringement, you might inquire with your technology consultant about the availability and cost of software that prevents others from copying the software. Another helpful technology is the ability to detect copying by searching the internet for content that is substantially similar to your content. One popular tool is found at http://www.copyscape.com/.

To help address pervasive copying of online works, the Digital Millennium Copyright Act ("DMCA") went into effect in 1988. The DMCA provides a process for removing unauthorized works from the internet. Specifically, the DMCA provides a safe harbor to internet service providers and website owners who did not directly infringe a third party's copyrights, did not have actual knowledge that the material was infringing, did not receive financial benefit directly attributable to the infringing activity and respond expeditiously to a proper notice to remove the material. [30]

To understand the DMCA, it is helpful to understand how the internet works. In order for a website to appear on the internet, several service providers are involved: (1) the website operator or owner (whoever actually *controls* the content on the website); (2) the internet service provider, which provides the website owner with access to the internet; and (3) the domain name registrar, which provides the uniform resource locator ("URL") or domain name to the website owner.

The website owner may or may not be directly responsible for posting the content. Often website owners actively post content on their website. However, many websites provide forums for third party postings, such as blogs and chat rooms. Some websites provide online publication services, where eBooks are published. A website owner is liable for copyright infringement if the owner or its agents directly post content on the website without permission that is copyright protected.

On the other hand, a website owner is *not* automatically liable for copyright infringement committed by a third party on its website. Under the DMCA, the website owner only becomes liable for third party content if it is put on notice of the infringement and fails to timely remove the content.

Similarly, the internet service providers ("ISP," also known as the host) is protected by the DMCA from liability unless it fails to disable access to infringing content after notice.

Domain registrars only register domain names and are never liable for copyright infringement on websites that they don't operate or host.

Thus, the DMCA serves the dual purpose of protecting the website owner from lawsuits for third-party copyright infringement and protects the copyright owner by providing the website owner an incentive to promptly remove infringing materials.

However, in order for a website operator to qualify for the safe harbor provisions of the DMCA, it must designate an agent who will receive DMCA notices. The designation is filed with the United States Copyright Office at copyright.gov. In 2017, The United States Copyright Office instituted an electronical registry and required all internet service providers to file new DMCA agent designations, even if they previously filed one. The filing is a simple form that can be found at copyright.gov and the filing fee is only $6.

In order to determine the identity of a website owner, you must perform a "whois" search. There are several resources for whois searches. A popular whois service can be found at www.whois.net. Another good resource is www.networksolutions.com (follow the "whois" link on the website). "Whois" will tell you who owns the website. There are, however, two problems that often arise. One is that the whois information may be phony. I have looked up whois information and found the owner to be John Smith with an address at 123 Main Street. Fortunately, there is a service for reporting false whois information. It can be found at http://wdprs.internic
.net. Following a report, the domain registrar must cause the website owner to correct the whois information. If the website owner fails to correct the deficiency, the domain registrar must take the domain name from the website owner.

A more difficult challenge is when the website owner has subscribed to a domain privacy service that makes its identity anonymous. In that case, you must direct your claims to the domain registrar that is providing the domain privacy service and follow their procedure for making any claims against the website owner.

If the infringing content that you want removed resides on a website operated by someone other than the infringer, you should utilize the DMCA process described below against the website owner to force the website owner to remove the materials. If the website owner is the infringer, he may be unwilling to remove the infringing materials. He may have intentionally stolen the content, which makes it likely that he has little regard for the law or your rights. In that situation, you will send your notice to the ISP. The ISP has the ability to control the website's access to the internet. The ISP is often confused with the domain name registrar. The domain name registrar has control of the web address, but not the content. The domain name registrar is not in a position to remove the website from the internet, even if the website is infringing your copyright. The ISP does have that control and will usually be responsive to a DMCA notice.

Once you have figured out whether you are directing your demands to the website owner or the ISP, you will next want to find out the specific person or email address to direct your notice. The United States Copyright Office website has a list of agents to whom DMCA notices should be sent. Every ISP or website owner that seeks protection under the DMCA must provide an agent name to the Copyright Office. If the website owner to whom you want to send a notice does not have an agent, you should send the notice to the "contact us" email address available on the website. In that case, the website operator or ISP may not have protection under the DMCA. Although anyone can send a DMCA notice, the notice must follow a strict format, and it is probably a good idea to utilize an attorney well-versed in copyright law to prepare and send the notice.

Typically, a properly prepared DMCA notice will result in prompt removal of the infringing material. Sometimes, dishonest website owners move the content to a new ISP rather than permit the ISP to block their access to the internet. In such cases, I send a DMCA notice to the new ISP and repeat the process until the website owner gets tired of moving from host to host.

Remember that the DMCA does not protect the intentional infringer. You may decide to send a DMCA notice to the ISP and also file a lawsuit against the website owner who intentionally copied your content. Also remember that a copyright must be registered before a lawsuit can be filed. A common plan is to submit the copyright application to the copyright office (if you had not already done so), send the DMCA notice or notices, wait for the copyright registration to issue, and then file the lawsuit if the infringement caused you substantial damages and/or did not stop after you sent a DMCA notice. If the infringement is causing you immediate and significant damages, you can also pay the copyright office for special handling to expedite your copyright registration. In some jurisdictions, you can file a lawsuit as soon as you file the application and need not wait until you receive the registration.

Although protecting online works can require diligence on your part, the laws and technological tools do make the task manageable. It helps to become familiar with the preventative measures available and, in the event of an infringement, to work closely with an attorney familiar with both intellectual property laws *and* internet laws.

Chapter 11
Contracts

As an author, it is important that you are knowledgeable about the formation of contracts and the types of contracts that you are likely to encounter in your work. Although the law of contracts is not complicated, people often misunderstand it.

A contract is nothing more than a legally enforceable agreement between two or more people or entities. To form a contract, there must be an offer, an acceptance of the offer and mutual consideration (something of value). Mutual consideration is required because the law will not enforce naked promises. If I offer to give you $1,000 and you accept the offer, we have not entered into a legally binding contract because the agreement lacks consideration. If I change my mind, you have lost nothing as a result of my indecisiveness.

As long as there is an offer, an acceptance of the offer and consideration, a contract does not generally need to be written. Oral contracts are usually enforceable but are not usually a good idea. Film producer Samuel Goldwyn said, "A verbal contract isn't worth the paper it's written on." The problem with a verbal contract is that human beings tend to perceive and/or remember conversations through the filters of our emotions and experiences. One thing that I learned very early in my career is that two witnesses who both believe they are telling the truth will almost always give a different description of the same conversation. If you rely on a verbal agreement, you are greatly increasing the chances of a dispute over the terms of the agreement. You are also risking that the other party may deny that the parties ever reached an agreement.

On the other hand, not every contract needs to be an attorney-authored, complicated, lengthy document. The hard part is knowing which deals can be verbal, which must be in writing, and which should be in a writing authored by an attorney. There is no standard formula or criteria to apply to such a decision. My personal opinion is generally that (1) a very basic agreement can be verbal; (2) an agreement that involves $5,000 or less in time, assets, or money can be in a writing drafted by the parties; and (3) agreements that involve more than $5,000 should be drafted (or at least reviewed) by an attorney. There are many attorneys who would disagree with me on this issue. Surely, the safe advice is that all contracts should be in writing and should be drafted by an attorney. Such advice, however, is not always practical or cost effective.

If you do enter into a verbal agreement, it is a good idea to send a letter or email to the other party describing and confirming the agreement. If you are entering into an agreement that is too small to justify hiring an attorney to draft or review, don't be intimidated by the task of drafting a contract. There is no required format to follow. The only requirement is to state the agreement in a clear and complete manner. You can even write a letter and ask the other party to sign their name at the bottom under the words "agreed and accepted."

Whether you are forming the agreement or documenting the agreement, you should identify what is expected of each party and identify what each party will receive in exchange for what they will provide to the other party. Write the agreement so that, in the event of a dispute, an uninvolved third party can understand the agreement. Avoid terms or phrases that the parties understand but a third party would not understand. For example, if you have a written agreement with a third party that states that you are licensing to that party the right to use a chapter in your book, identify the book with enough detail that there can be no dispute which book is being referred to. Also, you should make sure the written agreement is complete. If an item was discussed and an agreement was reached as to that item, include it in the written agreement.

A common mistake made by those who draft their own agreements is to confuse contracts with sales pitches. The contract is the not place to brag about how good your services are. By doing so, you are essentially legally promising the level of quality you claim in the contract.

Types of Contracts

While you might encounter a wide variety of contracts in your writing career, you are most likely to enter into certain types of agreements. Authors often enter into work for hire agreements, copyright assignment agreements, license agreements, publishing agreements, releases, and submission agreements. While some of these agreements were mentioned earlier, we will address each type of agreement in this chapter.

It is very important to keep in mind that within a category or type of agreement there can be a wide range of possible terms. Recently, a client called me and told me that he had entered into a publishing agreement several years earlier and that the publisher was no longer marketing the book. He asked me if he could take back the publishing rights. I teased him that my psychic powers were not working that day. My client had assumed that all publishing agreements have common elements and that I would know whether he could take back the rights. In reality, all contracts are different and there is no way I could know whether his publishing agreement had such a provision without reading it.

Confidentiality Agreements

Also, known as non-disclosure agreements or "NDAs," a confidentiality agreement simply states that one party to the agreement is providing the other party to the agreement with information that is confidential and that the receiving party agrees to keep the information confidential. Confidentiality agreements should be used whenever you need to share confidential information or trade secrets with another person. It is okay for non-disclosure agreements to be mutual when each party is sharing something confidential with the other party and they both agree to keep the other party's information confidential. But don't enter into a mutual confidentiality agreement when only one party is sharing confidential information. In that case, designate one party as the disclosing party and one as the recipient. A common misconception is that confidentiality agreements must have a time limit. That is simply not the case.

Authors often use confidentiality agreements to protect the plot or outline of a book or article before the writing is publicly available. Remember that if you want to keep something confidential, you should only share it on a "need to know" basis and anyone who needs to know, needs to sign a confidentiality agreement. For instance, you may need to share your book plot with an illustrator, a writing coach or a ghost writer. A well-written confidentiality agreement can make it clear to the recipient of your information how important it is to keep the information confidential and it will provide you with a legal remedy in the event that the recipient breaches that confidentiality.

Work for Hire Agreements

A work for hire agreement is a very simple form. The only tricky part is knowing when to use such an agreement. A properly written work for hire agreement results in someone other than the creator being the owner of copyright protected works.

You can use a work for hire agreement if you hire a third party to create (1) a contribution to a collective work (an article, column, or short story that has been published in a magazine, newspaper, or other periodical); (2) a part of a motion picture or other audiovisual work; (3) a translation; (4) a supplementary work; (5) a compilation; (6) an instructional text; (7) a test; (8) answer material for a test; or (9) an atlas.

The work for hire agreement will simply provide that Party A has paid (or will pay) Party B to create the work and that Party B is creating the work as a work made for hire to be owned by Party A.

It is customary to include a provision in a work for hire agreement that if the work is not considered a work for hire for any reason, Party B then assigns the copyright to Party A. This is a good idea in case the work is later determined to not fall into one of the nine categories listed above.

Copyright Assignments

A copyright assignment is also a simple form, or a simple provision contained within another contract. A copyright assignment transfers the ownership of a copyright-protected work to another person.

An author should carefully consider the consequences of assigning his or her copyright. Once you do so, you have no rights to continue to use the work for any purpose unless you receive permission or a license from the new owner. A common mistake that people make is thinking that because they were the original author of a writing, they can continue to use that writing even though they assigned the copyrights to a third party. Once you assign your copyright, you have no more right to use that work than someone who has no relationship to the new owner.

Whenever you sign any contract related to your works of authorship, be sure to review it carefully for any reference to assignment or transfer or the copyright. I am always amazed at how common it is for authors to be unaware of whether they assigned their copyright to a third party.

License Agreements

Whenever someone other than the copyright owner is commercializing a written work, there is either a license or there has been an infringement. In other words, the other party's use is either with permission, in which case it is a license, or without permission, in which case it is copyright infringement.

Licenses are not always in writing. If someone calls you and asks you for permission to reprint your poem, and you grant that permission, you have given a verbal license. The most common verbal licenses are between related parties. It is very common for authors who form small, closely-held, companies to verbally license their writings to the company so that the company can commercialize the works. It is a better practice to put those licenses in writing and pay fair market value for the license in order to keep the individual and the company separate from one another.

Anytime you are using someone else's materials (whether it is text, photographs, or graphics) you should enter into a license agreement that sets forth such details as how the works may be used, for how long the works may be used, where the works may be used and the compensation to be paid for use of the works.

License agreements are generally complex agreements that are drafted by attorneys, but in rare cases, the arrangement may be very straight forward, warranting a less formal agreement. For example, if I want permission to use a poem on the opening screen of a visual presentation for a one-time event, I might simply send an email asking permission and seek nothing more than the affirmative response of the author.

Publishing Agreements

Publishing Agreements are a specific type of license agreement. Typically, the publisher will present a standard agreement and expect authors to sign the agreement with little or no negotiation. Keep in mind that the publisher has likely had the agreement drafted by an attorney whose goal it is to protect the publisher's interests. It is important to have a publishing agreement reviewed by your own attorney. All too often, clients come to me after they have signed a publishing agreement and after they are unhappy with something that the publisher did. It is a far better practice to consult with an attorney to make sure the agreement meets your needs before you sign it.

A publishing agreement should identify the parties to the agreement. This sounds very basic, but it needs to be clear whether your publisher will distribute the book directly or through one of its affiliates or subsidiaries. The agreement should also properly identify the book or article that is being published. It is also important to describe the geographic area of distribution. I often see publishing agreements that give the publisher "worldwide" publishing rights even though the publisher has no intention of publishing outside the United States. As an author, resist permitting the publisher to tie up foreign rights unless the publisher demonstrates the ability and a willingness to exercise those rights.

The publishing agreement should also cover the various medium in which the work will be published. Here again, do not give rights beyond what the publisher has the ability and willingness to exploit. For instance, if the publisher is seeking the right to adapt the book into a screenplay, research whether that publisher has successfully done so in the past.

Of utmost importance, the publishing agreement will address the ownership of the copyright. It will either provide that the author retains the copyright and licenses the publishing rights to the publisher, or it will state that the author is assigning or transferring the copyright to the publisher. If the agreement provides for a license, it will address whether the license is exclusive and the scope of the exclusivity. An exclusive license means that only the publisher can publish the works during the time period of the agreement. I have had more than one client ask for my assistance after giving a long-term exclusive publishing agreement to a publisher who has become bored with the book and failed to market or distribute it for several years. Be sure to ask for a clause that releases the publishing rights back to you in the event the publisher fails to distribute an acceptable minimum number of books.

The publishing agreement will include a section where you represent and warrant to the publisher that you are the original author of the materials and that your writings have not violated the copyrights or other rights of any other party. This is a reasonable request that you should expect from the publisher.

The publishing contract may also address future works in the same series. It may or may not give the publisher the rights, or the first option to receive the rights to future works.

Of course, the publishing agreement will also cover compensation. You may enter into many different monetary arrangements. The contract should cover royalties on sales made by the publisher to others, sales made by the publisher to the author, and sales (if permitted) made by the author to others. The agreement will also cover when the payments are to be made (monthly, quarterly, semi-annually, or annually). It will address circumstances in which the royalty rates will be reduced, such as discounted sales. You should insist that royalty payments are accompanied by royalty statements that include enough details to understand how the publisher calculated the royalty payment.

While these are typical provisions found in a publishing agreement, there may be others or other variations. Because every publishing agreement is different, just knowing that there is a publishing agreement in place gives me little insight into the respective rights of the publisher and author. The only way to really know what you are getting into (or what you have gotten into) is to read the specific publishing agreement.

Releases

Releases are used to obtain permission to use someone else's name or likeness. They are closely related to licenses. Technically, it is an agreement to not sue someone, or not to pursue a legal claim. Without a release, your use of someone else's name or picture or photograph could result in that person suing you for defamation, violation of her privacy rights, or violation of her publicity rights. Releases are typically very short, very straight forward forms. *Getting Permission: How to License & Clear Copyrighted Materials Online and Off*, which is listed in the resources section of this book, includes simple, easy to understand release forms.

Submission Agreements

Publishers typically use submission agreements to protect them from claims by authors who submit works to them. Many publishers will not review or consider unsolicited submissions for fear that they will later be accused of infringement if they publish a similar work. Instead, they require the author to sign a submission agreement which includes the release of certain claims. The submission agreement usually appears on its face to include protection for the author in that it states that the publisher will not use the author's work without an agreement from the author. Of course, copyright law provides the same protection. But submission agreements typically contain terms that will make it difficult or impossible to sue the publisher for misappropriating story lines and plots. Sometimes, submission agreements state that by submitting the materials, you are transferring the copyright.

At the other end of the spectrum, you as the author may obtain a submission agreement from a publisher that broadens the rights you have as a copyright owner. An author-friendly submission agreement may provide that the publisher will not publish a book that embodies the plot or concept of your submitted story.

CONCLUSION

By now, you know more about intellectual property law than most general attorneys. I encourage you to keep this book and continue to use it as a resource when you encounter issues and questions.

While my intention was to touch upon the most common situations faced by authors, it would be impossible to predict and address every issue. If there are topics or situations that are not covered in this book that you would like to see addressed in future editions, please email me at mcs@jaburgwilk.com.

For more than twenty years I have taught classes at CEO Space on protecting intellectual property and internet law. If you would like to attend a workshop or seminar on the topics in this book, visit www.ceospace.net for more information about a week-long forum for entrepreneurs.

Sometimes the most important function of a guide such as this is to identify the areas where the reader should seek personal, custom-tailored advice. Since there are many nuances in the law and because many laws are intentionally left to interpretation, you should seek legal advice for your specific situation. Also, anytime anyone is entering into a relationship with another party that involves a substantial expense, time commitment, or risk, the terms of the agreement between the parties should be in writing. Such agreements should be drafted or at least reviewed by an attorney skilled in that particular field.

For information and articles on other areas of intellectual property and internet law, please visit our website at www.jaburgwilk.com. Watch for future books in this series, including the following anticipated titles:

➢ Protect Your Photographs: A Legal Guide for Photographers

➢ Protect Your Art: A Legal Guide for Artists and Graphic Artists

➢ Protect Your Music: A Legal Guide for Composers and Musicians

➢ Protect Your Code: A Legal Guide for Software and Web Developers

➢ Protect Your Plays: A Legal Guide for Playwright

➢ Protect Your Architectural Designs: A Legal Guide for Architects

About the Author

Maria Crimi Speth is a shareholder in the law firm of Jaburg & Wilk, P.C. Ms. Speth practices in the areas of intellectual property, internet law, and commercial litigation, representing clients throughout the United States. She focuses her practice on assisting businesses in protecting their trademarks, copyrights, trade secrets, information technology, and other intellectual property through preventative measures to avoid disputes and through litigation when disputes arise.

Ms. Speth received her B.A., cum laude in 1985 from Hofstra University and received her J.D. in 1988 from Hofstra University School of Law. She is admitted to practice in the State of Arizona Supreme Court, the Appellate Division of the Supreme Court of the State of New York, the United States District Court for the District of Arizona, the United States District Court for the Eastern District of New York, the United States District Court for the Southern District of New York, the United States Court of Appeals for the Ninth Circuit, the United States Court of Appeals for the Federal Circuit, the United States Court of Appeals for the Eleventh Circuit, the United States Court of Appeals for the Seventh Circuit, the United States Court of Appeals for the First Circuit, and the Supreme Court of the United States of America.

Ms. Speth has authored articles on the topics of litigation and intellectual property, published in The Business Journal, the Arizona Journal of Real Estate & Business, and the Arizona Attorney. Her profile has been featured in the Arizona Business Gazette and The Herold Report.

In October of 2000, the readers of Arizona Women's News voted Ms. Speth best business attorney in Arizona. In April of 2008 she was listed in the Top Lawyers list published by Arizona Business Magazine. She is a certified member of The Million Dollar Advocates Forum and a member of The American Trial Lawyer's Association Top 100 Trial Lawyers in Arizona and America's Top 100 High Stakes Litigators.

Ms. Speth is a past chair of the intellectual property section of the Arizona State Bar Association. She is on the Board of Directors of the Metropolitan Phoenix YWCA, a non-profit organization whose mission is empowering women and eliminating racism.

Ms. Speth has presented seminars for the State Bar of Arizona, the Arizona Small Business Association, The Inventors' Association of Arizona, National Business Institute, and Lorman Education Services. She is on the faculty of the internationally acclaimed CEO Space. She has also been a guest speaker on television and radio shows addressing intellectual property protection topics.

Resources

The official website of the United States Copyright Office: www.copyright.gov

The website of CEO Space entrepreneurial forums: www.ceospace.net

The official website of the United States Patent & Trademark Office:
www.uspto.gov

Getting Permission: How to License & Clear Copyrighted Materials Online and Off by Attorney Richard Stim

Charts to calculate when works pass into the public domain:

https://www.copyright.cornell.edu/publicdomain

http://www.unc.edu/~unclng/public-d.htm

INDEX

END NOTES

1   Uniform Trade Secret Act

2   35 U.S.C. Section 154

3   35 U.S.C. Section 101

4   35 U.S.C. Section 101

5   Circular 1, Copyright Basics, United States Copyright Office

6   Circular 1, Copyright Basics, United States Copyright Office

7   17 U.S.C. Section 106(3); Circular 1, Copyright Basics, United States Copyright Office

8   17 U.S.C. Section 101; Circular 9, Works Made For Hire Under the 1976 Copyright Act, United States Copyright Office

9   *Community for Creative Non-Violence v. Reid*, 490 U.S. 730 (1989).

10   Circular 9, Works Made For Hire Under the 1976 Copyright Act, United States Copyright Office

11 The Dummy Series is a registered trademark of John Wiley & Sons, Inc.

12 As of the date of writing, there was a split in the circuits as to whether a pending application is enough for filing a lawsuit or whether the plaintiff must have a registration. The U.S. Supreme Court is expected to resolve the split.

13 Circular 1, Copyright Basics, United States Copyright Office

14 Circular 1, Copyright Basics, United States Copyright Office

15 17 U.S.C. Section 407

16 Circular 7b, "Best Edition" of Published Copyrighted Works for the Collection of the Library of Congress, United States Copyright Office

17 17 U.S.C. Section 102(b)

18 17 U.S.C. Section 107

19 American *Geophysical Union v. Texaco, Inc.*, 60 F.3d 913 (2d Cir. 1995)

20 Statement of Marybeth Peters, The Register of Copyrights, before the Subcommittee on Courts, the Internet, and Intellectual

Property, Committee on the Judiciary, March 13, 2008

[21] 17 U.S.C. Section 105

[22] 17 U.S.C. Section 101

[23] Creativecommons.org/about/what-is-cc

[24] Restatement (Second) of Torts Section 652A

[25] Restatement (Second) of Torts Section 652D

[26] *Haelan Laboratories, Inc. v. Topps Chewing Gum, Inc.*, 202 F.2d 866 (2d Cir.) *cert. denied* 346 U.S. 816 (1953).

[27] McCarthy, *The Rights of Publicity and Privacy* 1:3.

[28] California Civil Code Section 3344

[29] *Playboy Enterprises, Inc. v. Welles*, 279 F.3d 796 (9th Cir. 2002)

[30] 17 U.S.C.A. §512

Made in the USA
Middletown, DE
02 February 2024

49026726R00080